"In *Building Bridges*, Fazale Rana, Anjeanette Roberts, and Jeff Zweerink build a strong case from physics, chemistry, and biology that the universe is best explained as the purposeful creation of an intelligent designer. The intricacies of design described throughout this book far exceed those proposed by William Paley when he argued in 1802 that a complex watch would certainly require an expert craftsman. Evidence of a designer is demonstrated in such diverse subjects as the big bang, DNA, human uniqueness, and even viruses. The scope and depth of evidence presented in this short book should be enough to challenge any purely naturalistic explanation for our universe."

–Michael G. Strauss, PhD
David Ross Boyd Professor of Physics
The University of Oklahoma

"Science is a universal 'language' that gives powerful evidence for God. Additionally, this evidence strongly supports that the biblical description of who God is, his character, and his relationship to us is true. In *Building Bridges*, the authors provide convincing evidence from cosmology, chemistry, biochemistry, genetics, evolutionary biology, etc., that God exists and that we can know and understand more about him by examining nature and the Bible. Science, as the authors so wonderfully demonstrate, is a 'bridge' between peoples of many varying beliefs, and is also a bridge to the validity of the Bible. *Building Bridges* is a wonderful and very encouraging book to read."

–Russell W. Carlson
Professor Emeritus
Department of Biochemistry & Molecular Biology
Complex Carbohydrate Research Center
University of Georgia

"*Building Bridges: Presentations on RTB's Testable Creation Model* is accessible both to those who have a scientific background, and those who do not. Drs. Rana, Roberts, and Zweerink do an excellent job of addressing some of the key questions when it comes to the evidence for a creator; one who is a loving, caring God made known through nature. They achieve this by addressing topics such as cosmology, evolution, biochemistry, and to me most intriguing of all—why God created viruses. Each chapter is a self-contained unit and can serve as the launching point for further in-depth study; a bibliography being provided for the reader. The 'personal touch' is also weaved through the book, each author explaining some of their own faith journey. The book particularly appeals to me because it provides useful nuggets of information I can use in conversation with non-Christian friends and colleagues, and starting points for discussion with Christians who see science and faith as being at odds with one another. It is also a real faith-builder for me personally."

–Nicholas E. Leadbeater
Associate Professor
Department of Chemistry
University of Connecticut

D0838698

"How wide is the scope of a Christian worldview? Does it encompass scientific philosophy, theory, and interpretation? In six compelling and beautiful essays, taken from lectures given at an inter-faith conference held recently in Istanbul, the authors answer this question resoundingly in the affirmative. From the fine-tuning of the universe to the transcendent design evident in the DNA or the vital and beneficial role of viruses for life on the Earth, these essays masterfully illustrate how a Christian picture of creation is in deep harmony with our scientific experience, so long as we are willing to shed the blinders of philosophical naturalism."

–Bijan Nemati
Principal Research Scientist
University of Alabama in Huntsville

"With *Building Bridges*, Rana, Roberts, and Zweerink once again demonstrate their ability to present the case for creation in a way that is at the same time both irenic and biblically faithful. Christians and people of other religions often cooperate in matters of ethics and moral commitments. Rana and company show that there are similar opportunities in the scientific realm, particularly concerning the evolution/creation controversy. And although the contents of this book were originally presented and discussed in the context of a Christian/Muslim dialogue, a person with no religious convictions will find the arguments contained to be enlightening and compelling."

–Kenneth Keathley
Director of the L. Russ Bush Center for Faith and Culture
Professor of Theology
Southeastern Baptist Theological Seminary

"If you sense a growing urgency to reach the Muslim community with the truth about Jesus, you might be surprised to find that *science and technology* can help you begin a conversation about the nature of God and the truth of Christianity. In their new book, *Building Bridges: Presentations on RTB's Testable Creation Model*, Fazale Rana, Anjeanette Roberts, and Jeff Zweerink provide an approach for engaging Muslims that is rooted in a shared goal—the promotion of *creationism*. If you want to understand how science and Christianity can coexist and how Reason to Believe's testable creation model can help you find common ground with your Muslim neighbors, I highly recommend *Building Bridges: Presentations on RTB's Testable Creation Model*."

–J. Warner Wallace
Cold-Case Detective
Senior Fellow at the Colson Center for Christian Worldview
Adjunct Professor of Apologetics at Biola University
Author of *Cold-Case Christianity*, *Cold-Case Christianity for Kids*,
God's Crime Scene, and *Forensic Faith*

"For anyone wondering whether science can show us if God exists, or whether science and Christianity can mutually support each other, I highly recommend this book for its affirmative answer to these questions. This book offers an easily readable introduction and rich survey of multiple lines of evidence from nature which point to its Creator. *Building Bridges* will open the reader's eyes to the glory of God!"

–John A. Bloom, PhD
Chair, Chemistry, Physics and Engineering Department
Biola University
Founder and Academic Director
Master's Degree in Science and Religion Program
Biola University

"In *Building Bridges*, authors Rana, Roberts, and Zweerink do the reader a great service by compiling in one place thoughtful scientific commentary on questions of origins (the universe, life, and humans). As professional scientists, they have the technical knowledge to provide a substantive look at each issue; however, they also make the material accessible to the reader. Particularly interesting is Roberts's chapter on virology. Her exposition shows the amazing fine-tuning discoverable in the realm of ecology. Overall *Building Bridges* is another solid offering from the scientists at RTB."

–J. Thomas Bridges, PhD
Academic Dean and Professor of Philosophy
Southern Evangelical Seminary

"In *Building Bridges: Presentations on RTB's Testable Creation Model*, Fazale Rana, Anjeanette Roberts, and Jeff Zweerink have written a book which truly excites me. Why? Because it models the very best of scientific expertise in the service of Christ. First, the eminently readable chapters are taken from lectures the three presented in Istanbul, Turkey, to build bridges with their largely Muslim audience. Second, the chapters are so well-written that I would love to give this to scientifically minded westerners who doubt the relevance of Christianity today. Third, I think the book will boost the faith of Christians who have wondered how to relate their faith to science. Thanks to Rana, Roberts, and Zweerink for this gem!"

–Ted Cabal, PhD
Professor of Apologetics
The Southern Baptist Theological Seminary
General ed., *The Apologetics Study Bible*
Coauthor *Controversy of the Ages: Why Christians Should Not Divide over the Age of the Earth*

"This book is filled with facts that make great conversation-starters. Fascinating findings about biology, computers, viruses, cells, and the nature of the universe itself. No philosophical premises in it discount the vast complexity of the cosmos. Each scientist speaks as a scientist. None evade the science by making sweeping religious claims. All three writers carefully explain their respective research, then show the logic of taking seriously the biblical account of creation."

–Sarah Sumner, PhD, MBA
President of Right On Mission

FAZALE R. RANA
ANJEANETTE ROBERTS
JEFF ZWEERINK

BUILDING BRIDGES

PRESENTATIONS ON RTB'S TESTABLE CREATION MODEL

Covina, CA

© 2018 by Reasons to Believe

All rights reserved. No part of this publication may be reproduced in any form without written permission from Reasons to Believe, 818 S. Oak Park Rd., Covina, CA 91724.
reasons.org

Cover design: Sean Platt
Interior layout: Christine Talley

Unless otherwise identified, all Scripture quotations taken from the Holy Bible, New International Version ®, NIV®. Copyright ©1973, 1978, 1984, 2011 by Biblica, Inc.™ Used by permission of Zondervan. All rights reserved worldwide. www.zondervan.com The "NIV" and "New International Version" are trademarks registered in the United States Patent and Trademark Office by Biblica, Inc. ™ Scripture quotations marked (NLT) are taken from the Holy Bible, New Living Translation, copyright © 1996, 2004, 2007, 2013, 2015 by Tyndale House Foundation. Used by permission of Tyndale House Publishers, Inc., Carol Stream, Illinois 60188. All rights reserved.

Rana, Fazale, 1963-, author | Roberts, Anjeanette, author. | Zweerink, Jeff, author.
Building bridges : presentations on RTB's testable creation model / Fazale Rana; Anjeanette Roberts; Jeff Zweerink.
Includes bibliographical references and index. | Covina, CA: RTB Press, 2018.
ISBN 978-1-886653-08-5
LCSH Religion and science | Intelligent design (Teleology) | Church and the world. | Islam--Relations--Christianity. | Christianity and other religions--Islam. | BISAC RELIGION / Religion & Science | SCIENCE / Cosmology
LCC BL240.2 .R32 2018 | DDC 215--dc23

Printed in the United States of America

First edition

1 2 3 4 5 6 7 8 9 10 / 22 21 20 19 18

For more information about Reasons to Believe, contact (855) REASONS / (855) 732-7667 or visit reasons.org.

To Amy: Thank you for selflessly supporting me in my efforts to use science to build a bridge to the Christian faith.

–FR

To all who claim Christ and seek to follow him, may we always build bridges to the Risen Lord.

–AR

For Lisa Zweerink and our five beautiful children.

–JZ

Contents

List of Figures

Acknowledgments

There are many people who worked hard and sacrificed to make *Building Bridges* possible.

First, we want to thank members of the Technics and Science Research Foundation for hosting and inviting us to speak at the first and second International Conferences on the Origin of Life and the Universe. Specifically, we want to thank Mr. Adnan Oktar, Dr. Oktar Babuna, Dr. Cihat Gündoğdu, Mina Berkmen, Mrs. Zuhal Mansfield, Serra Basarir, Selda Oktän, Burcu Çekmece, Said Uğur, Ali Sadun, Omar Mosheni, and Alkaz Cakmak for your hospitality and friendship.

We especially want to acknowledge the editorial team at Reasons to Believe who dedicated themselves to this book as if it were their own. Thank you, Joe Aguirre, Sandra Dimas, Jocelyn King, and Maureen Moser for your expert editorial guidance. Your efforts transformed our draft manuscript into a book that we are proud to call our own. Thanks to Colleen Wingenbach for proofing the manuscript and Sean Platt for designing the book cover. Also thanks to Christine Talley for designing the interior layout of the book.

We are indebted to our fellow scholars at Reasons to Believe. Thanks to Drs. Hugh Ross and David Rogstad and to Kenneth Samples for many insightful conversations in the hallway and during lunch. These discussions helped to directly and indirectly shape the contents of this book. Thanks to Drs. Michael Strauss and Sarah Sumner for their critical reading of the manuscript. Your input helped improve the technical accuracy and clarity of the book.

We are also grateful to each member of the Reasons to Believe team. You have supported us with your friendship and encouragement through the years. We are honored to call you friends. We are also grateful to Kathy and Hugh Ross for their friendship and guidance. You have had a profound and lasting influence on each of our lives.

Establishing Common Ground with People of Different Faiths

Fazale R. Rana, PhD

It sounds cliché, but we live in a shrinking world. And whether we like it or not, we now find ourselves immersed in a global society. It's not uncommon to encounter people whose faith differs from our own—or people with no faith at all. Our interactions aren't just online. They include face-to-face exchanges with coworkers and neighbors, as people from all over the globe move to the Western world. As Christians, we desire to build friendships with people who see the world differently than we do. Along the way, we want to help our new-found friends understand Christianity and why we believe it's true. But how do we develop friendships? How do we introduce Christianity to people who hold disparate worldviews?

In my experience, friendships develop most readily where common ground exists. And once friendships exist, interesting, meaningful conversations about faith often follow. At Reasons to Believe (the organization where Anjeanette "AJ" Roberts, Jeff Zweerink, and I all work), we think science and technology provide fertile ground for building friendships between Christians and people who embrace a secular worldview. Most nonreligious people believe that science helps us discover the truth about the world around us. They also regard technology as the pathway that can help bring an end to human suffering. As Christians, we believe the same thing. The Old and New Testaments teach us that God has made himself known to us through his creation—through nature. We believe evidence for God's handiwork and character can be found as we investigate the world through science. In other words, we believe that science helps us understand the world in which we live, and in doing so points the way to the Creator. We also believe we have been given a divine mandate to be stewards of the planet and to use what we learn from science to develop technology that promotes human flourishing and provides the means to treat those who suffer from diseases and injuries. Though Christians may interpret some scientific insights differently than secular scientists, ample opportunity exists for believers and nonbelievers to find common ground in the scientific arena.

But what about people who hold to religious worldviews, yet come from different faiths? How can we build bridges with them? What common ground exists?

Often, Christians strive to find points of connection with people of other religions by emphasizing our shared moral commitments. But, as AJ, Jeff, and I discovered in Istanbul, science and technology can also serve as common ground for Christians and Muslims. In fact, it can even motivate cooperative efforts. Both Muslims and Christians believe that a transcendent, personal being brought the universe and life into existence. And many Christians and Muslims see the evolutionary paradigm as a challenge to God's existence and role in bringing about life's origin, history, and design. Given these connecting points, that's where the three of us hoped to begin building bridges.

Building Bridges in Istanbul

Straddling the continents of Europe and Asia, Istanbul is one of the world's most fascinating cities.

A boat ride along the beautiful Bosporus strait, which separates the Asian and European parts of the city, provides stunning panoramic views. Both shorelines are heavily settled, crowded with modern amenities crammed alongside centuries-old buildings. Three bridges span the Bosporus to connect Asia and Europe: the 15 July Martyrs Bridge, the Fatih Sultan Mehmet Bridge, and the brand-new Yavuz Sultan Selim Bridge (completed in 2016). At night, brightly colored lights adorn all three bridges, making the view from the boat quite dramatic.

When walking the lively, colorful streets of Istanbul the influences of Europe and the Middle East become apparent, particularly in the food and architecture. The food is an amazing amalgam, drawing inspiration from neighboring cultures such as Greece and the Middle East. Each meal starts with colorful vegetable salads, followed by perfectly grilled meats and savory stews.

Orthodox churches and mosques pepper the Istanbul cityscape, some even standing side-by-side. In fact, some mosques were once Orthodox churches. For instance, the magnificent Hagia Sophia began as the Roman Empire's first Christian cathedral in the fifth century AD, was converted into a mosque in the mid-1400s following conquest by the Ottoman Empire, and is now a museum. The history of the building's origin, takeover, and transition can be seen on its walls and ceilings.

International Conferences on the Origin of Life and the Universe

Though Istanbul (and indeed all of Turkey) brings Christianity and Islam into juxtaposition, somehow the adherents of both religions have learned to live peacefully and productively together. Perhaps it's no surprise then that AJ, Jeff, and I were invited to Istanbul to speak at both the first and second International Conference on the Origin of Life and the Universe (held in August 2016 and May 2017, respectively). Sponsored by the Technics and Science Research Foundation (TSRF), these meetings featured Christian and Muslim scientists and scholars collaborating to present a scientific case for God's existence, and they highlighted scientific challenges to the evolutionary paradigm. Through these conferences, TSRF intended to build a bridge between Christians and Muslims by demonstrating that it is possible for the two groups to work cooperatively toward a shared goal—namely promotion of creationism—despite significant and profound religious differences.

AJ, Jeff, and I accepted the invitation to speak at the first conference. We viewed our time in Istanbul as an unprecedented opportunity to present a Christian perspective on creation to audiences comprised largely of Muslims. We also saw it as a chance to build our own bridges of friendship with Muslim scholars. We believed a shared interest in defending creationism would serve as a structural framework to support the bridge. AJ and I returned to the second conference to continue the building process.

Through our interactions, we realized that many Muslims don't fully understand Christianity. And many Christians don't understand Islam. Our common ground as creationists allowed us to have open, enlightening, and entertaining conversations with our new friends and conference attendees about the similarities and differences between the two faiths.

Both conferences were truly international in scope. The lectures were simultaneously translated into English, Turkish, and (for the second conference) Italian. Each speaker had to provide written transcripts of his or her presentation to the translators. Later, the three of us realized that, as a result of producing our transcripts, we had generated a collection of essays surveying our Reasons to Believe (RTB) creation model. The topics span the origin and design of the universe to the origin, history, and design of life—including the origin of humanity.

The Reasons to Believe Creation Model

This book presents the essays taken from our Istanbul lectures. Though edited for publication here, each chapter remains true to the content shared in our conference presentations.[1] Each chapter stands alone, making it easy to skip around, if desired. At the same time, the lectures build on one another to make an overarching scientific case for the Christian faith.

In the opening chapter, Jeff Zweerink presents the foundation of the RTB creation model. He describes how scientific evidence for the universe's beginning and the fine-tuning of the universe's fundamental constants, parameters, and characteristics can be used to marshal a case for God's existence and the scientific credibility of the Bible's cosmology.

In chapter 2, I explain why I, as a biochemist, believe God exists based on the latest insights from origin-of-life research, biochemistry, and synthetic biology. In chapter 3, I describe how work in nanotechnology can be leveraged to make a case for the Creator. I focus specifically on the elegant, ingenious, and optimal design of DNA.

A frequent challenge to biological design and the case for the Creator looms in the problem of pain and suffering. Nothing exemplifies this issue better than viruses. In chapter 4, AJ addresses viruses by offering a theologically and scientifically rich explanation as to why an all-good, all-powerful, and all-knowing God would include viruses in creation.

In chapter 5, AJ explains different definitions for the term "evolution." Understanding the different usages of "evolution" can go a long way in addressing the claim that there is more evidence for evolution than evidence that the earth revolves around the Sun.

Finally, in chapter 6, I address human evolution by arguing that the most compelling evidence for human evolution (the hominid fossil record and shared genetic similarities between humans and the great apes) can be easily accommodated within a creation model framework. I also point out some nagging scientific problems confronting human evolution. I conclude the chapter by touching on recent discoveries in molecular genetics and archaeology that support the biblical account of human origins.

Is This Book for You?

Rest assured, you need not be a scientist or a theologian to benefit from the essays in this book. Are you curious to see if science and Christianity can exist in harmony? Are you curious about RTB and our old-earth creation approach to science-faith issues? If so, these written lectures are ideal for you.

These essays are not exhaustive, but they are an accessible introduction to some of the most important facets of RTB's creation model. And if your interest is piqued after reading one or more of the lectures, each chapter includes a list of relevant RTB resources (books, articles, and videos) that invite you to dig deeper.

Are you uncertain whether Christianity is true? Do you believe the biblical creation accounts are incompatible with scientific evidence? These essays are ideal for you, too.

They provide an expansive case for God's existence from cosmology and biology. They also provide reasons why we, as scientists, think the Bible's creation accounts are scientifically credible and why we think the Christian worldview provides a powerful framework for understanding the natural world, including pain and suffering.

Do you believe there is no need for God because evolutionary mechanisms can explain the origin, history, and design of life? This book uses scientific rationale to demonstrate that evolutionary mechanisms come up short, particularly regarding the origin and design of life.

Keep in mind that, in an effort to maintain readability and accessibility for a wide audience, we intentionally kept references to original scientific literature to a minimum. If you want to verify our claims and check out the scientific evidences for yourself (and we encourage you to do so), then we invite you to read the articles and books listed in the resource section of each chapter. These resources provide detailed lists of scientific references that support our model.

Are you curious about how Christian scholars would present a distinctly Christian perspective on creation to a Muslim audience in an Islamic country? These written lectures are for you. Because of the context in which the lectures were presented, each essay presents scientific evidence for God's existence and identifies scientific challenges to the evolutionary paradigm that would resonate with both Christians and Muslims. In some places, we use language accessible to a Muslim audience rather than common Christian wording. Even so, our essays retain a distinctly Christian perspective on creation.

As this collection of written lectures demonstrates, we at RTB believe that science is an effective way to build a bridge to the Christian faith. Science can be used to establish a strong point of connection between Christians and secularists. And after our experiences in Istanbul, we believe that Christians can use science and technology to build bridges into the Islamic world, too, providing ways to help Muslims understand Christianity.

If you desire to share the profound uniqueness of the Christian faith with anyone—whether they are skeptics or people of different faiths—nothing is more effective than establishing friendships first. We hope that these written lectures will inspire you to build your own bridges.

 ## Resources to Dig Deeper

Hugh Ross, *More than a Theory: Revealing a Testable Model for Creation* (Grand Rapids: Baker Books, 2012).

Hugh Ross, *A Matter of Days: Resolving a Creation Controversy*, 2nd expanded ed. (Covina, CA: RTB Press, 2015).

Hugh Ross, *Navigating Genesis: A Scientist's Journey through Genesis 1–11* (Covina, CA: RTB Press, 2014).

Chapter 1

The Origin and Design of the Universe

Jeff Zweerink, PhD

Prominent atheist cosmologist Lawrence Krauss is fond of making statements like this:

> The amazing thing is that every atom in your body came from a star that exploded. And, the atoms in your left hand probably came from a different star than your right hand. It really is the most poetic thing I know about physics: You are all stardust. You couldn't be here if stars hadn't exploded, because the elements—the carbon, nitrogen, oxygen, iron, all the things that matter for evolution—weren't created at the beginning of time. They were created in the nuclear furnaces of stars, and the only way they could get into your body is if those stars were kind enough to explode. So, forget Jesus. The stars died so you could be here today.[1]

Obviously, Krauss's statement is specifically antagonizing to Christians, but I think it is offensive to *all* religions that believe in a God who created the universe and all it contains. Krauss argues that science can explain everything; therefore, we don't need a god.

However, as a Christian who is a scientist I come to a different conclusion. A theistic worldview provides the best explanation of our scientific understanding of the universe. Let me say that again: a *theistic* worldview provides the best explanation of our scientific understanding of the universe. The evidence for this conclusion is plentiful, but here I'll share just three powerful examples.

In the Beginning

At the start of the 1900s, three significant features characterized scientists' understanding of the universe. First, the universe was eternal and had existed forever. Second, the universe was static and unchanging on the largest scales. And third, as one moved through the universe the laws of physics changed in subtle ways. Before describing how twentieth-century scientific advances changed this picture, I want to contrast this early scientific view with the Bible's description.

Starting in Genesis 1 we see that God created the heavens and the earth. In this account, God brought the universe into existence out of nothing. In other words, the universe had a beginning; it has not existed forever. Other prophets also speak about the nature of the universe. For example, Isaiah records God describing himself as the "Maker of all things, who stretches out the heavens . . . by myself" (Isaiah 44:24). Not only does this text affirm a beginning for the universe, it also implies that the universe is dynamic on the largest scales rather than static and unchanging.

What might be most important scientifically is a statement the prophet Jeremiah recorded. According to Jeremiah 33:25, God declares that "if I have not made my covenant with day and night and established the laws of heaven and earth," then he would break his promises and not fulfill what he said he would do. Although this passage refers to how objects move through the heavens, we now know that this motion ultimately depends on constant laws of physics! So Jeremiah is describing a universe where the laws of physics are constant, which is a critical criterion for the development of the scientific enterprise. Note the contrast between the early twentieth century's scientific picture of the universe and the one revealed by God. A little more than 100 years ago, scientists thought the universe was eternal, static, and governed by changing laws of physics. God revealed that the universe is temporal, dynamic, and governed by constant laws of physics.

So let's take a look at some of the important discoveries that brought the scientific picture in line with the theistic one described by the Bible. During the 1910s, Albert Einstein recognized that in the scientific description of the day, the laws of physics changed as one moved through the universe. Philosophically, he didn't like that idea. So he set about developing a model of the universe where the laws of physics were constant. In doing so, he developed the special theory of relativity and the general theory of relativity. The key feature of these theories is that the laws of physics are constant and unchanging regardless of how you're moving or where you're located in the universe. Scientists have thrown numerous experimental tests at the theory of general relativity to see if it is valid or not, and it has passed every test with outstanding success. It is one of the best-established and best-accepted scientific theories known today.

One consequence of general relativity, when you solve its equations, is that the universe ought to be dynamic, either contracting or expanding. Initially, Einstein didn't like this idea, but measurements in the 1920s and 1930s ultimately established that the universe is indeed expanding. Edwin Hubble looked out at what he called island universes (we now call them galaxies) and found that the farther away a galaxy was, the faster it was moving away from us. This is a telltale signature of an expanding universe. General relativity predicted an expanding or dynamic universe, and measurements of these distant galaxies show that the universe *was* expanding. If it's expanding, then perhaps if you run time backwards there was a beginning.

Scientists resisted this idea for quite some time, and they looked for numerous ways to retain the concept of an eternal universe. But in the 1960s, with the measurement of the cosmic microwave background radiation, Stephen Hawking, Roger Penrose, and other scientists developed some very powerful theorems. These theorems showed that if general relativity describes the dynamics of the universe accurately (and it has passed every test we have thrown at it) and if the universe contains mass (and we're pretty sure of that), then we can draw the conclusion that when you run time backwards the universe has a boundary. In other words, the universe began to exist.

So, at the close of the twentieth century, the scientific view of the universe looked very much like a theistic worldview thanks to significant scientific discoveries. *We live in a universe that began to exist. The universe is expanding. And constant laws of physics govern the universe.* These are the three essential features of all big bang models. In other words, the universe that God revealed to us through the Bible matches the universe that we see when we study creation.

In recent years, scientists have proposed multiverse models—where our universe is just one of a great ensemble of universes. Some people argue that the multiverse challenges the notion of the beginning. However, even the existence of an inflationary multiverse affirms the conclusion that the universe began to exist.

The first piece of scientific evidence supporting a theistic worldview is that inflationary big bang cosmology shows that the universe began to exist. This conclusion supports the second premise of the kalam cosmological argument that, in syllogism form, says:

> Whatever begins to exist has a cause;
> the universe began to exist;
> therefore, the universe has a cause.

Fine-Tuned Coincidences

The second major support for the existence of a creator is the pervasive evidence of design in the universe. Such evidence appears throughout the universe, from the laws of physics to the genetic code.

Consider what it takes for humanity to live. For starters, we (and indeed all organisms) require carbon, water, and a planet where liquid water can exist in the presence of abundant carbon. Many of the scientists studying the universe's ability to support life come to the conclusion that the universe looks like it was designed to do so. Even self-professed atheists and agnostics have acknowledged the appearance of design. Atheist astronomer Fred Hoyle said, "A common sense interpretation of the facts suggests that a superintellect has monkeyed with physics, as well as with chemistry and biology. . . . The numbers one calculates from the facts seem to me so overwhelming as to put this conclusion almost beyond question."[2]

It is no controversy to say that the best scientific evidence indicates that the universe appears designed for life, and we see that evidence across the scientific disciplines. Let's take a look at some of the universe's features that look designed to support life.

Fine-Tuned Dimensions

We live in a universe with three large spatial dimensions and one time dimension, but we can analyze what would happen if the dimensions were different. For example, what if there were only *two* spatial dimensions? As it turns out if there were two or fewer spatial dimensions, then the universe would not be complicated enough for life. Imagine an animal in two dimensions. If the animal has a passage for food intake and a different passage for expelling waste, in two dimensions such passages would cut the animal in half. Now you could make an argument that the food could come back out the same way, but such an argument misses the point. In two dimensions there are not enough ways physically to make connections in order to have the complexity life requires.

Perhaps more dimensions would be better. It turns out that if you go to four, five, or more spatial dimensions, there are no stable orbits. With more spatial dimensions, atoms are not stable and planets either spiral into their host star or fly into space. Thus, the critical requirements for life—elements and planets—don't exist. Changing the number of time dimensions creates even worse problems. Anything more or less than one time dimension leads to a situation where physics is unpredictable. Now you may say, "I don't know how to do physics, so why is it necessary for it to be predictable?" It so happens that "physics being predictable" is a foundational requirement for life. Every organism must be able to sense the environment, tell what has occurred in the past, and determine what will happen in the future. However, if physics is *un*predictable, this is impossible. Life can exist only in a universe with three large spatial dimensions and one time dimension.

Fine-Tuned Physics
Let's turn our attention now to the laws of physics; especially at how carbon, oxygen, and hydrogen exist in the universe. According to big bang cosmology, in the first four minutes of the universe's beginning only hydrogen and helium (and trace amounts of lithium and beryllium) existed. All the elements heavier than these are formed inside stars. As scientists studied how well stars produce carbon and oxygen, they found huge deficiencies of these elements unless some remarkable coincidences were true. In particular, the difficulty of producing carbon is that three helium nuclei have to come together at the same time. Because it's a three-body interaction, that makes the process very slow. However, as scientists looked more closely they recognized two important factors that allow the formation of carbon.

First, when two helium atoms come together they can form a beryllium-8 nucleus. Beryllium-8 is not stable, but it does stick around for a while. This means that only one more helium nucleus needs to collide with the beryllium-8 in order to form carbon, which speeds up the reaction considerably. However, even with the metastable beryllium-8 nucleus, stars would not produce enough carbon. Something else was missing. In the 1950s Fred Hoyle, one scientist working on the problem, recognized a solution that would produce carbon rapidly enough. If carbon had a particular energy level just above the ground state (or the lowest energy state) the reaction would proceed more quickly. At the time carbon was not known to have this particular energy level, but subsequent study by Hoyle and others showed that such an energy level existed. Without a stable beryllium-8 nucleus and a finely tuned energy level for carbon, the universe would not produce sufficient carbon for life.

Yet in order for the universe to contain sufficient carbon, oxygen's energy level must be fine-tuned, too. If oxygen had an analogous energy level, then all carbon would fuse into oxygen, leaving no carbon. Fortunately, oxygen does not have this energy level. These coincidences show that the universe contains large amounts of carbon *and* large amounts of oxygen, both of which are critical for life.

Although I've used the word "coincidence" to describe these essential features, I think it is more accurate to say that the universe was *designed* to produce the elements necessary for life. It was the discovery of the exquisite balance of the laws of physics that prompted Fred Hoyle to acknowledge the appearance of design.

Similar design features also ensure the universe has the necessary hydrogen for life. For example, if two protons could join together and form a stable nucleus, the universe would have used up all the hydrogen in the first few minutes after its creation. The same thing would have happened if there were any stable five-nucleon elements or eight-nucleon elements. The strength of the fundamental laws of physics determines whether these design features exist or not. If we plot the strength of the electromagnetic interaction against the strength of the strong nuclear interaction, then we can ask the question: where in this space can life exist? The answer is that only a very small region of the available parameter space meets all the necessary requirements for life. This feature points to design, that there is a creator who fashioned the universe for a purpose.

Fine-Tuned Moon
Looking a little closer to home we see evidence of design in the Moon that orbits Earth. Jupiter and Saturn both have satellites that are larger than Earth's Moon. However, when compared to the size of the host planet, Earth's Moon is in a class by itself. The Moon's large size plays an important role in Earth's capacity to host life. For example, without such a large moon to maintain stability Earth's rotation axis would wobble, causing violent and catastrophic changes to our climate. Perhaps more importantly, the size of the Moon helps provide the heat necessary to enable plate tectonic activity on Earth for billions of years. The gravitational tug of the Sun and the Moon causes Earth's interior to flex, stretch, and compress. This tugging heats up Earth's interior, and that heat drives the plate tectonic activity. As scientists seek to understand how Earth acquired such a large moon they recognize that it took a remarkable collision early in Earth's history. This collision needed to happen at the just-right speed, at the just-right time, at the just-right angle, with an object of the just-right size. It really is an unusual collision. It looks like the Moon was designed so that Earth can support life.

Fine-Tuned Genes

A third piece of evidence for fine-tuning comes from biology. DNA is commonly called the blueprint of life. It is made up of four compounds represented by the letters T, C, A, and G. These letters come in groups of three and each group specifies the production of an amino acid. Sequences of three letters where each letter has four options mean there are 64 different possibilities. Yet because only 20 different amino acids are involved in life, this means that different combinations of three will produce the same amino acid. Likewise, the amino acid sequences determine how proteins will fold and sometimes different amino acids will still produce the same protein folding.

Scientists can then ask the question: how well does the genetic code ensure that the proteins fold and function properly even with mutations in the specific letters? Given the redundancy in amino acid coding and the similarity of amino acids in protein folding, scientists have determined that our genetic code is literally one in a million in its ability to minimize errors caused by mutations. Additionally, the genetic code resides at a global optimum (not just the best in a given range, but the best overall). Such exquisite fine-tuning reminds me of a statement by Francis Crick, co-discoverer of the iconic DNA double helix. He said, "Biologists must constantly keep in mind that what they see was not designed, but rather evolved."[3]

I disagree. When scientists look at the universe they see evidence of fine-tuning and design at all scales. They see fine-tuning in the fabric of space-time, in the form and strengths of the laws of physics, in the size of our Moon, in the genetic code, and in many other areas I have not mentioned. It seems natural to conclude that when we see design it is because a designer exists and created the universe to support humanity.

The Philosophical Foundations of Science

Inflationary big bang cosmology shows that the universe began to exist. Science also shows that the universe looks like it was designed for life to exist. Now let's look at the third piece of evidence pointing to God's existence: the foundations of the scientific enterprise.

No one disputes the utility of science. We have discovered great things about this universe, and we have developed great resources and technology to benefit humanity. In order for science to work, though, every scientist must operate under a specific set of philosophical assumptions. For example, a scientist must believe that the laws of nature are uniform throughout the physical universe. If the laws were not uniform then no measurements made here on

Earth would apply to the universe as a whole. Without uniform physical laws, the scientific enterprise would have never even gotten started.

A scientist must also assume that the physical universe is a distinct and objective reality. Contrast this view with Hinduism, for example, where the physical world is ultimately an illusion. If the world were an illusion why would we go about studying it and trying to understand how it works?

Additionally, a scientist must assume that the laws of nature exhibit order, patterns, and regularity. I am reminded of my studies of Greek mythology in school. Greek mythology is littered with gods and goddesses who are arbitrary and capricious. One day they're bestowing gifts and favors, the next they're angrily stirring up oceans or throwing lightning bolts. If this were the worldview a scientist has about the universe, then why would he or she expect to see any sort of order, regularity, and pattern in nature?

In order for science to work the physical universe must also be intelligible. Those patterns and order must be sensible and understandable in some way. Also, the world itself must not be divine; otherwise, the proper response would be to worship it, not treat it as an object of rational study. Again, I think of the Eastern mystical religions or the "basic" religions as they're called. In these worldviews, the physical is divine and mystical, and our goal is to become one with nature, not to study it and figure out how it works.

Another assumption the scientist makes is that the world is good, valuable, and worthy of study. In college, I read a story about Siddhartha Gautama, the Buddha. During the course of the story, Siddhartha ultimately gained genuine enlightenment—perfection, the sought-after goal—through detachment from the world. He learned that the world is not good, but rather it gets in the way of the true goal. If detachment from the world is the ultimate goal, why would we try to understand the way the world works?

Productive, successful scientists must also assume that the universe could be different. In other words, if the Creator has free agency, then he could have chosen to do things differently. That's why we must study and experiment to figure out what was done. A theistic view of the world not only encourages the scientific enterprise but also compels humanity to study creation. In Genesis, God issues an imperative to Adam and Eve to take dominion over nature. Moreover, God's moral law grounds and encourages essential intellectual virtues such as honesty, integrity, a good work ethic, and many others.

One final assumption a scientist must make in order to do good science is that humans possess an ability to discover the universe's intelligibility. If humans did not have this ability, then it would make no difference whether the universe met all the assumptions listed previously or not. The scientific enterprise would never have gotten started. Consider what atheistic naturalism has to say about humanity's ability to reason and understand. If atheistic naturalism is true then humanity's primary purpose is simply to survive. No reason exists to think that human thought could comprehend how the universe works. C. S. Lewis describes the atheist's conundrum very well:

> If the solar system was brought about by an accidental collision, then the appearance of organic life on this planet was also an accident, and the whole evolution of Man was an accident too. If so, then all our present thoughts are mere accidents— the accidental by-product of the movement of atoms. And this holds for the thoughts of the materialists and astronomers as well as for anyone else's. But if their thoughts—i.e. of materialism and astronomy—are merely accidental by-products, why should we believe them to be true? I see no reason for believing that one accident should be able to give me a correct account of all the other accidents.[4]

Given these foundational principles of science, one should then ask the question: what worldview(s) properly anchors all of these philosophical presuppositions? Atheistic naturalism cannot. Buddhism and Hinduism cannot. Eastern religions and Greek mythology cannot. But a theistic worldview— where God creates humanity with a purpose and a moral code and a desire to worship and know God—can and does. I am *not* saying that a scientist must be a theist in order to do science, but I *am* saying that a scientist must adopt the worldview of a theist for the scientific enterprise to progress consistently and endure over time.

Many vocal researchers claim that science falsifies the notion of a God and justifies an atheistic belief. However, a close inspection of the latest scientific evidence provides strong evidence that God exists. Throughout the Bible, multiple authors describe a universe that began to exist, is governed by constant laws of physics, and that expanded over time. Inflationary big bang cosmology affirms that we live in a universe matching this description—*even if* our universe is part of a larger multiverse. Our universe shows exquisite fine-tuning for life to exist. It looks designed for life! Only a theistic worldview anchors all the essential philosophical foundations required for science. Not only does the scientific evidence demonstrate the rationality of belief in God, I would argue that God's existence provides the best explanation of our scientific understanding of the universe.

 ## Resources to Dig Deeper

Hugh Ross, *The Creator and the Cosmos: How the Latest Scientific Discoveries Reveal God*, 3rd expanded ed. (Colorado Springs, CO: NavPress, 2001).

Hugh Ross, *Navigating Genesis: A Scientist's Journey through Genesis 1–11* (Covina, CA: RTB Press, 2014).

Jeff Zweerink, *Who's Afraid of the Multiverse?* (Glendora, CA: Reasons to Believe, 2008).

Fazale Rana, *The Cell's Design: How Chemistry Reveals the Creator's Artistry* (Grand Rapids: Baker Books, 2008).

Kenneth Samples, *Without a Doubt: Answering the 20 Toughest Faith Questions* (Grand Rapids: Baker Books, 2004).

Jeff Zweerink, "Most Persuasive Scientific Reason to Believe?," *Impact Events* (blog), *Reasons to Believe*, February 3, 2017, reasons.org/explore/blogs/impact-events/read/impact-events/2017/02/03/the-most-persuasive-scientific-reason-to-believe.

Jeff Zweerink, "Persuasive Reasons: Thoughts on Fine-Tuning," *Impact Events* (blog), *Reasons to Believe*, March 10, 2017, reasons.org/explore/blogs/impact-events/read/impact-events/2017/03/10/persuasive-reasons-thoughts-on-fine-tuning.

Jeff Zweerink, "Multiverse Musings—A Matter of Faith?," *Today's New Reason to Believe* (blog), *Reasons to Believe*, March 26, 2008, reasons.org/explore/publications/tnrtb/read/tnrtb/2008/03/26/multiverse-musings---a-matter-of-faith.

Fazale Rana, "The Genetic Code: Simply the Best," *Today's New Reason to Believe* (blog), *Reasons to Believe*, July 2, 2007, reasons.org/explore/publications/tnrtb/read/tnrtb/2007/07/02/the-genetic-code-simply-the-best.

Kenneth Samples, "Statements about Science That Bother Me, Part 3," *Today's New Reason to Believe* (blog), *Reasons to Believe*, May 27, 2008, reasons.org/explore/publications/tnrtb/read/tnrtb/2008/05/27/statements-about-science-that-bother-me-part-3.

Chapter 2

Why I Believe God Exists:
A Biochemical Case for the Creator

Fazale R. Rana, PhD

Does God exist? What role does science play in answering this vital question? Do scientific advances eliminate the need for a creator—or do they, in fact, undermine the evolutionary paradigm so often used to justify atheism?

These questions are important for Muslims and Christians, alike.

If evolutionary mechanisms can account for the origin and history of life and the design of biological systems, then it is right to ask if there is any role for a creator to play. In his book *The Blind Watchmaker*, evolutionary biologist and atheist Richard Dawkins notes, "Although atheism might have been logically tenable before Darwin, Darwin made it possible to be an intellectually fulfilled atheist."[1]

Statements like this cause many people to conclude that conflict exists between science and religion and science will eventually win the war. In August 2015, the Pew Research Center published data showing that almost 75 percent of Americans who never or seldom attend church believe there is conflict between science and faith. Unfortunately, this same survey showed that 50 percent of regular church attendees believe the same.[2]

And yet, it was science that led me to the strong conviction that a creator must exist. When I entered college, I was an agnostic. I didn't know if God existed or not, and, honestly, I didn't really care. Religion did not interest me. Instead, my attention centered on biochemistry. I was eager to prepare myself for graduate school so that I could earn a PhD in my chosen field.

As an undergraduate, I became convinced that evolutionary mechanisms could account for the origin, history, and design of biological systems. My convictions were not based on a careful examination of the evidence, but rather on what my biology professors taught me. I admired them; thus, I accepted their claims about the evolutionary paradigm without hesitation. In many ways, my misplaced confidence in evolutionary explanations fueled my agnosticism. To-day, when I speak on university campuses in the United States I often encoun-ter students who, like me, embrace the evolutionary paradigm without criti-cism because they, too, respect and admire their professors.

But my views changed during graduate school. You might say that bio-chemistry convinced me that God must exist. One of the primary goals of a graduate education is to teach students to think independently through the scientific evidence and to develop conclusions based on the evidence alone, regardless of what other experts might say. Because I was learning to think for myself, I was willing to ask questions that I had not voiced as an undergraduate. The elegance, sophistication, and ingenuity of biochemical systems prompt-ed me to ask, "How did life originate?" I wanted to know how the scientific community could account for the origin of such remarkable systems through strictly mechanistic processes.

After examining the various explanations available at that time (this was 30 years ago), I was shocked. The scientific community's explanations seemed woefully inadequate. I was convinced that chemical and physical processes alone could not generate life. This realization, coupled with the elegant design of biochemical systems, forced me to the conclusion—for intellectual reasons alone—that a creator must indeed exist and must have been responsible for bringing life into being.

That was over 30 years ago and in the subsequent decades the scientific evidence has continued to affirm my convictions about God's existence. The case for a creator from the design of biochemical systems and the problems as-sociated with the origin of life have become even more compelling.

The goal of this chapter is to present the reasons why, as a biochemist, I think God must indeed exist. My argument can be summarized using three keywords:

1. Fingerprints: A creator's fingerprints are evident in biochemical sys-tems.
2. Failure: All avenues taken to explain the origin of life through chemical evolution have resulted in failure.
3. Fashion: Attempts to create and fashion life in the lab make a powerful case for a creator.

Fingerprints

When human beings design, create, and invent systems, objects, and devices, we leave behind telltale signatures in our creations that reflect the work of a mind. As a biochemist, I find it remarkable that the hallmark features of the cell's chemical systems are identical to those features that we would recognize as evidence for the work of a human designer. If specific features reflect the work of human intelligence, and we see those very features in the cell's chemical makeup, then is it not reasonable to conclude that intelligent design undergirds life itself?

Signatures of intelligent design abound in the cell. I simply cannot discuss all of them here. Instead, I would like to focus on the information systems found inside the cell.

Biochemical Information Systems

At their essence, biochemical systems are information systems. Two classes of biomolecules harbor information: (1) the nucleic acids, such as DNA and RNA; and (2) proteins. Both types of molecules are chain-like. These molecules are formed when the cell's machinery links together smaller, subunit molecules in a head-to-tail fashion to form molecular chains. In the case of DNA and RNA, the subunit molecules are called nucleotides. In the case of proteins, the subunit molecules are called amino acids. Twenty different amino acids are encoded within the genetic code. The cell's machinery uses these twenty amino acids to construct proteins.

Biochemists often think of nucleotides and amino acids as molecular alphabets. (Nucleotides are sometimes referred to as the genetic letters abbreviated A, G, C, and T.) Just as alphabet letters are used to construct words in English or Turkish, so amino acid sequences are used to construct biochemical words—proteins—that carry out specific functions inside the cell. Nucleotide sequences are used to store information in DNA. In fact, DNA's chief function is to store information that the cell's machinery uses to build proteins. The regions of the DNA molecule that house this information are called genes.

The recognition that biochemical systems are information systems indicates that a creator generated life. Why? Because our common experience teaches us that minds generate information. When you receive a text message or when you see a sign along the side of the road, you invariably conclude that someone composed those messages in order to communicate information to you. In like manner, it is reasonable to conclude that a divine mind generated the cell's information systems.

Organized Information

But the case for the Creator does not rest on the mere existence of biochemical information. The argument is much more sophisticated. As it turns out, information theorists studying problems in molecular biology conclude that the *structure* of the cell's information systems is identical to the organization of human language. Again, it is not solely the presence of information in the cell, but the way in which that information is organized that points to purposeful design.

One of the most provocative scientific insights I have ever learned relates to the structure and function of biochemical information. Computer scientists and molecular biologists have come to realize that the cell's machinery, which manipulates DNA, literally functions like a computer system at its most basic level of operation. Because this insight is so important to the case for a creator, I would like to spend more time developing the concept. To do so, we need to consider the work of British mathematician Alan Turing.

Turing Machines and the Cell

One could argue that Turing ranks among the most important scientists of the twentieth century. And yet, until a few years ago, most people did not even know who he was. Recently, Turing's vital work in the effort to crack the Nazi Enigma code during World War II garnered fresh attention when the British government released classified information from that time period. It turns out that Turing was a war hero. He, along with other cryptanalysts based at Bletchley Park (50+ miles north of London), designed and operated electromechanical machines used to break Enigma. Historians have estimated that these efforts may have shortened the war by two years and saved about 14 million lives.

As if his contributions to the British war effort were not substantial enough, Turing is also considered by many to be the father of modern computer science. Prior to the war and after it, Turing produced theoretical work that heavily influenced the theoretical framework for modern-day computer science. Much of the technology we enjoy today traces its origin, in part, to theoretical insights that flowed out of Turing's mind.

Part of Turing's theoretical construct for computer systems were abstract machines, known today as Turing machines. These abstract entities existed solely in Turing's mind. Turing machines are very simple, consisting of three components: (1) the input, (2) the finite control, and (3) the output.

The input is a string of data that flows into the finite control. The finite control operates on the data string in a prescribed manner, altering it and generating an output string of data. The finite control can perform only limited operations on the data string. Turing's genius was to recognize that the output of one Turing machine could become the input to another. In this way, an ensemble of Turing machines can be combined in numerous ways to perform numerous, distinct, complex operations.

This is precisely the same way that the cell's machinery manipulates genetic information. Information housed in DNA is digital information. Whenever a complex biochemical process (such as DNA replication) takes place, the cell's machinery—in the form of proteins—takes the digital information in DNA as input, alters it in a prescribed manner, and produces an output strand of digital genetic information. The individual proteins serve as the finite control. While each protein can perform only a limited transformation of the DNA information, by working in combination with other proteins, more complex biochemical operations ensue. In other words, when the cell's machinery replicates DNA, it is essentially carrying out a computer operation.

DNA Computing
The similarity between cellular processes and the fundamental operation of computer systems has inspired a brand-new area of nanotechnology called DNA computing. This cutting-edge field is the brainchild of computer scientist Leonard Adleman of the University of Southern California. Adleman proposes that DNA computing paves the way for a new understanding of life:

> The most important thing about DNA computing is that it shows that DNA molecules can do what we normally think only computers can do. This implies that Computer Science and Biology are closely related. That every living thing can be thought to be computing something, and that, sometimes, we can understand living things better by looking at them as computers.[3]

DNA computers are made up of DNA and the proteins that manipulate this biomolecule. These "bio-computers" are housed in tiny test tubes, yet they are more powerful than the most advanced super computer system we have available to us. That power stems largely from their capacity to perform a vast number of parallel computations simultaneously.

DNA computing highlights the remarkable similarities between human designs and the biochemical designs inside the cell. We can use these astounding similarities to construct a formal argument for God's existence by following in the footsteps of British natural theologian William Paley.

Divine Watchmaker

In 1802, Paley wrote a book called *Natural Theology* in which he advanced the watchmaker argument, which went on to become one of the best-known arguments in the West for God's existence. In a nutshell, Paley reasoned that just as a watch requires a human watchmaker, so life requires a divine watchmaker.

In Paley's day, a well-made watch exemplified expert craftsmanship. Paley pointed out that a watch is a contrivance—a machine composed of several parts that interact precisely to accomplish its purpose. He then contrasted a watch with a stone. A stone, Paley argued, finds explanation through the outworking of natural processes; but a watch requires a mind to explain its existence. Based on a survey of biological systems, Paley concluded that living systems have more in common with the watch than with a stone. And if a watch requires a human watchmaker to explain its existence, then by analogy, living systems require a divine mind to explain their existence.

Advances in biochemistry allow us to bring the watchmaker argument into the twenty-first century. We know from common experience that computer systems—the pinnacle of engineering achievement in our day—require a mind (in fact, many minds) to explain their existence. And because we find computer systems operating within the cell, we can reasonably conclude that life requires a divine mind to account for its existence.

I find the watchmaker argument compelling. Yet in my experience when I present this argument to skeptics they often argue that evolutionary processes can serve as the watchmaker. In fact, many evolutionists, such as Dawkins, regard these processes as the blind watchmaker. Dawkins articulates this idea in his book:

> [Paley] had a proper reverence for the complexity of the living world, and he saw that it demands a very special kind of explanation. The only thing he got wrong was the explanation itself. ... The true explanation ... had to wait for ... Charles Darwin. ... Natural selection, the blind, unconscious, automatic process which Darwin discovered, and which we now know is the explanation for the existence and apparently purposeful form of all life, has no purpose in mind. It has no mind and no mind's eye. It does not plan for the future. It has no vision,

no foresight, no sight at all. If it can be said to play the role of watchmaker in nature, it is the blind watchmaker.[5]

Dawkins' challenge brings us to the second point of my argument for God's existence.

Failure

To account for the origin of biochemical systems within the evolutionary paradigm, researchers must appeal to a set of processes dubbed chemical evolution, which is the "blind watchmaker" of biochemical systems. But, as I will show, every attempt to explain the genesis of biochemistry via chemical evolution has resulted in frustration and failure.

To appreciate how severe this problem is we need to review the way in which biochemists categorize the different types of biochemical systems. Biochemists frequently organize biochemical systems into three categories: (1) information-rich molecules (proteins and nucleic acids), (2) intermediary metabolism, and (3) cell membranes. (We have already discussed information-rich biomolecules such as proteins and nucleic acids.)

Intermediary metabolism refers to the collection of chemical reactions involving small molecules that take place inside the cell. These chemical reactions are organized into a series of pathways in which one molecule is converted into another molecule. The pathways can be linear, branched, or cyclical. Often, the pathways will intersect with each other to form a highly reticulated ensemble of chemical reactions. These chemical pathways are critical for harvesting energy for the cell's use. They are also used to make the building blocks that form DNA, RNA, proteins, and the constituents of cell membranes, and to process molecular waste secreted from the cell.

Cell membranes form boundaries that separate the interior of the cell from the exterior environment. Membranes also form compartments within the cell's interior.

Chemical Evolution Models

These three categories of biochemical systems have inspired corresponding models for chemical evolution: (1) replicator-first, (2) metabolism-first, and (3) membrane-first.

According to replicator-first scenarios for the origin of life, the first biochemical systems centered on information-rich molecules and it was only later in the evolutionary process that metabolism and cell membranes emerged. In like manner, metabolism-first scenarios envision metabolic systems emerging first and, finally, for membrane-first scenarios cell membranes arise first.

It is important to realize that each approach to the origin of life suffers from intractable problems. For example, the replicator-first approach suffers from the monomer problem, the homochirality problem, and the homopolymer problem. (Because of space constraints, I cannot detail these problems here. AJ Roberts discusses some of them in chapter 5.)

Many origin-of-life researchers readily acknowledge these profound issues. In 2002, I attended the International Society for the Study of the Origin of Life in Oaxaca, Mexico. The conference attracted some of the best origin-of-life scientists, including the late Leslie Orgel. When he was alive, Orgel was considered the preeminent origin-of-life researcher in the world. Because of his status, Orgel was given the honor of opening the conference with a lecture in which he offered his perspective on the RNA world hypothesis. This idea, which Orgel himself conceived, is considered the most important idea in origin-of-life research. Yet throughout his lecture, Orgel detailed problem after problem with the RNA world hypothesis. Toward the end of his talk, he paused, then said, "I hope that there are no creationists in the audience, but it would be a miracle if a strand of RNA ever appeared on the primitive Earth."[6]

It was remarkable. Orgel was known as an outspoken atheist, yet in an honest moment he acknowledged that the origin of life requires a miracle—at least when envisioned as a replicator-first scenario. As I point out in *Creating Life in the Lab*, Orgel's conclusion still holds today.

Metabolism-First Models
Metabolism-first scenarios fare no better. They are susceptible to disruption due to chemical interference and proceed too slowly to be effective means of generating life.

The scenario is also dependent on transport mechanisms and on mineral catalysts (but mineral surfaces have limited catalytic range). Before Orgel died, he described metabolism-first scenarios as "an appeal to magic," "a series of remarkable coincidences," and "a near miracle."[7] Again, Orgel's conclusion still holds. (See *Creating Life in the Lab*.)

Membrane-First Models
And finally, membrane-first scenarios are also riddled with problems. These models require exacting environmental conditions, amphiphile composition, amphiphile concentration, and phase behavior. Plus, the requirements for each

step in these scenarios are incompatible.

A few years ago, chemist Jackie Thomas and I published a paper detailing the problems with membrane-first scenarios, in the journal *Origins of Life and Evolution of Biospheres*. In my view, this was a remarkable achievement. Both Thomas and I are creationists. And yet the problems we identified with membrane-first scenarios are so significant, even evolutionary biologists had to acknowledge that our critique was legitimate. The editor-in-chief of the journal consented to publish our critical assessment of membrane-first scenarios in the premier origin-of-life publication.

In other words, every attempt to explain the origin of life has resulted in failure. There is no blind watchmaker.

Honest skeptics will agree that—as of now—we do not have an explanation for the origin of life. However, in my experience, when presented with critiques of chemical evolution scenarios, skeptics often argue that chemists have identified numerous chemical and physical processes in the laboratory that could conceivably contribute to the origin of life. They claim that these insights constitute important clues as to how life emerged through chemical evolution. For example, they will highlight such laboratory successes as:

- the synthesis of most "building block" molecules
- production of biopolymers
- evolution of functional RNA molecules
- generation of self-replicating systems
- manufacture of protocells

This response leads us to the third component of our argument for God's existence.

Fashion

When chemists go into the lab and perform prebiotic chemistry studies they are working under highly controlled conditions. They carefully assemble the glassware and fill it with the appropriate solvents. They add the just-right chemicals at the just-right time and just-right concentrations. They control the reaction's temperature and pH. And they stop the reaction at that just-right time.

In other words, the chemists are contributing to the success of the prebiotic chemistry studies. It is highly questionable whether such tightly controlled conditions existed on early Earth. To put it another way, intelligent agency ensures the success of prebiotic reactions in the lab.

Let me illustrate this point by discussing the RNA world hypothesis. The centerpiece of this idea is the notion that the very first biochemistry on Earth was RNA-based. (Later, the RNA world evolved to give rise to the DNA/protein world that characterizes contemporary biochemistry.) Origin-of-life researchers highlight several lines of evidence in favor of the RNA world hypothesis. I'm going to discuss just one of them.

Creating RNA Molecules in the Lab

In the mid-1990s, scientists in the lab observed RNA molecules assembling on clay surfaces from chemical building blocks. This observation was heralded as a huge breakthrough for the RNA world hypothesis. It meant that RNA could conceivably form on early Earth with an assist from clays and other minerals. Yet when the RNA assembly experiments are examined, it becomes evident that intelligent agency was critical to ensure the success of this chemical process.

For example, the researchers who performed the studies excluded materials that would interfere with RNA assembly on clay. These disruptive materials most certainly would have been present on early Earth. Researchers also were very careful to exclude materials that would promote the breakdown of RNA molecules. Such materials most certainly would have been present on early Earth. The team also stopped the reaction before the RNA molecules got too long and became irreversibly attached to the clay surface. When that happens, the RNA molecules will no longer be available for subsequent steps in the origin-of-life process. There would not have been organic chemists on early Earth to stop the chemical reaction before the RNA became permanently bound to the clay.

Additionally, the researchers had to use chemically activated building blocks to make the RNA molecules on clay. These activated building blocks would not have been present on early Earth. And if they were, they would be so reactive that they would have reacted with all kinds of materials before they could form a strand of RNA. Lastly, the scientists had to buy the clay they used in their experiments from a specific supplier and then still had to treat the clay in the lab to remove all the ions except for sodium.

It is ironic that the very experiments that have been performed to demonstrate that chemical evolution could explain the origin of life drive us to the conclusion that intelligent agency is required for life to originate from a complex chemical mixture. Astrobiologist Paul Davies had this to say in response to these experiments:

As far as biochemists can see, it is a long and difficult road to produce efficient RNA replicators from scratch. . . . This conclusion has to be that, without a trained organic chemist on hand to supervise, nature would be struggling to make RNA from a dilute soup under any plausible prebiotic conditions.[8]

Evolutionary biologist Simon Conway Morris said:

. . . many of the experiments designed to explain one or other step in the origin of life are either of tenuous relevance to any believable prebiotic setting or involve an experimental rig in which the hand of the researcher becomes for all intents and purposes the hand of God.[9]

These conclusions are affirmed by work in the relatively new discipline called synthetic biology.

Creating Life in the Lab

One of the goals of synthetic biology is to construct artificial cells in a laboratory setting. When one examines the work in synthetic biology, it becomes apparent the necessary role intelligent agency plays in transforming simple chemical materials into protocells. Let me illustrate this point by looking at what it takes to make a single enzyme, which would serve as one minor component in the cell's machinery.

A few years ago, a research team sought to make an enzyme that performed a chemical reaction not found in biological systems. In addition to biochemists and molecular biologists, the project needed a team of quantum chemists, computational chemists, and protein engineers. It required not just these skilled scientists but also hundreds of hours of supercomputer time, use of structural motifs from proteins in nature, and sophisticated instrumentation.

The work of these researchers can rightly be considered science at its very best. And yet when their enzyme was compared to the enzymes typically found in biological systems, their accomplishment was laughable.

Although our results demonstrate that novel enzyme activities can be designed from scratch and indicate the catalytic strategies that are most accessible to nascent enzymes, there is still a significant gap between the activities of our designed catalysts and those of naturally occurring enzymes.[10]

Divine Watchmaker Revealed
It seems the watchmaker isn't blind at all. To summarize, we made a case for God's existence by showing that:

1. A creator's fingerprints are evident in biochemical systems;
2. All avenues taken to explain the origin of life through chemical evolution have resulted in failure; and
3. Attempts to create and fashion life in the lab make a powerful case for a creator.

It is gratifying to me that the reasons that convinced me to believe in a creator 30 years ago are still valid today. In my view, if one is truly open to the evidence at hand, there is only one conclusion: a creator must exist and must be responsible for bringing the very first life-forms into existence. And if a creator is responsible for the origin of life, then it is reasonable to think that the history of life stems from that creator's handiwork as well.

 Resources to Dig Deeper

Fazale Rana and Hugh Ross, *Origins of Life: Biblical and Evolutionary Models Face Off* (Covina, CA: RTB Press, 2014).

Fazale Rana, *The Cell's Design: How Chemistry Reveals the Creator's Artistry* (Grand Rapids: Baker Books, 2008).

Fazale Rana, *Creating Life in the Lab: How Discoveries in Synthetic Biology Make the Case for a Creator* (Grand Rapids: Baker Books, 2011).

Chapter 3

The Inspirational Design of DNA

Fazale R. Rana, PhD

As I argued in chapter 2, the latest insights from origin-of-life research, biochemistry, and synthetic biology can be marshaled to make a case for a creator and, at the same time, raise challenges to the evolutionary paradigm.

The goal of this essay is to show how work in nanotechnology expands upon the scientific argument for God's existence. Toward this end, I will focus on the elegant, ingenious, and optimal design of DNA. More and more, researchers are finding that DNA is precisely engineered for its role in the cell as a molecular-scale information storage system. The structure and function of this biomolecule is so highly optimized that it is inspiring technology development in digital data storage media, computing, and nanoelectronics.

The use of biological designs to drive technological advancement is one of the most exciting areas in engineering. This discipline—called *biomimetics and bioinspiration*—presents us with new reasons to believe that life stems from a creator and, at the same time, raises fundamental problems for the evolutionary paradigm.

DNA's Role in the Cell

To appreciate how DNA can inspire advances in nanotechnology, it is important to understand the role this biomolecule plays in the cell. DNA functions chiefly as an information storage system. The cell's machinery uses the digital information built into the structure of the DNA molecule to produce proteins—the molecules used to form the cell's structures and carry out the cell's operations.

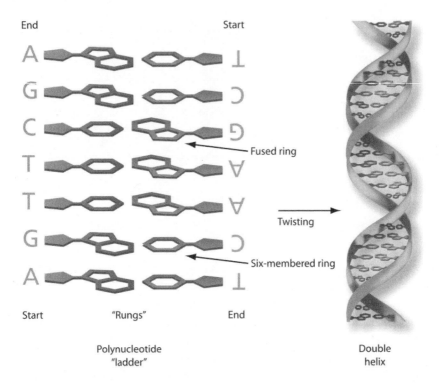

End   Start

A

G

C   Fused ring

T

T   Twisting

G   Six-membered ring

A

Start   "Rungs"   End

Polynucleotide   Double
"ladder"   helix

Figure 3.1: DNA Structure

DNA consists of chainlike molecules that twist around each other forming the well-known DNA double helix. The polynucleotide chains of DNA are formed from four different nucleotides—adenosine (A), guanosine (G), cytidine (C), and thymidine (T).

DNA's Structure

DNA consists of chain-like molecules known as polynucleotides. Each polynucleotide is formed by linking together two of four different subunit molecules called nucleotides—adenosine (A), guanosine (G), cytidine (C), and thymidine (T). Two polynucleotide chains align in an antiparallel fashion (meaning they run in opposite direction alongside one another) to form a DNA molecule. The two strands are arranged alongside one another with the starting point of one strand (the 5' end) in the polynucleotide duplex located next to the ending point of the other strand (the 3' end) and vice versa. The paired polynucleotide chains resemble a ladder with the side groups extending from the backbone to form rungs. The coupled polynucleotide chains twist around each other to form the well-known DNA double helix.

Protein Production

DNA stores the information necessary to make all the proteins used by the cell. The sequence of nucleotides in DNA strands that specifies production of a specific protein is known as a gene.

Proteins are "workhorse" molecules. They take part in essentially every cellular and extracellular structure and activity. Some proteins help form structures inside the cell and in the cell's surrounding matrix. They are dissolved in the cytosol (liquid inside the cell) and the lumen (interior space) of organelles or they aggregate to form larger structures like the cytoskeleton. Structural proteins also associate with the cell membrane in a variety of ways.

Proteins called enzymes catalyze chemical reactions. Enzymes are perhaps the most important type of protein. These biomolecules speed up the rate of chemical transformations by bringing the molecules together so they can react more readily. Other proteins harvest chemical energy, serve in the cell's defense systems, and store and transport molecules—and these are only a few of the roles that proteins play.

How Genetic Information Flows

The central dogma of molecular biology describes how information stored in DNA becomes functionally expressed through proteins. DNA does not leave the nucleus to direct the synthesis of proteins. Rather, the cellular machinery copies the gene sequence by assembling messenger RNA (mRNA), a single-stranded polynucleotide. (Scientists refer to this copying process as transcription.) Messenger RNA is similar, but not identical, in composition to DNA.

Once transcribed from the DNA, mRNA migrates from the nucleus into the cytoplasm. At the cell's ribosome, mRNA directs the synthesis of proteins. The information content of the polynucleotide sequence is translated into the protein's amino acid sequence. The protein then folds into a precise three-dimensional shape.

DNA's Optimal Structure and Features

As biochemists have studied the properties of DNA, they have come to appreciate that this molecule is optimally designed as a molecular-scale data storage system. In fact, biochemists think that DNA approaches the theoretical maximum in terms of its digital data storage capacity.

Two key properties are necessary for DNA to store information: (1) molecular stability and (2) protein binding. It is through protein binding that the information in DNA is accessed and DNA replication proceeds. Protein

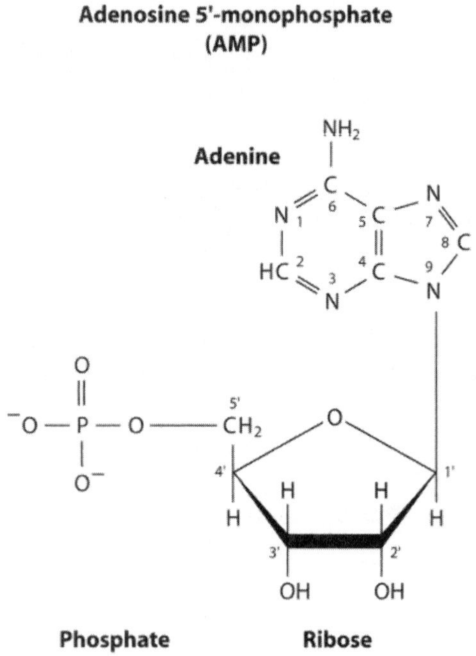

**Adenosine 5'-monophosphate
(AMP)**

Figure 3.2: Nucleotide Structure

The subunit molecules that make up the strands of DNA and RNA consist of both a phosphate moiety and a nucleobase (either adenine, guanine, cytosine, or thymine) joined to a five-carbon sugar (deoxyribose). In RNA, deoxyribose is replaced with the five-carbon sugar ribose.

binding also allows DNA repair to take place.

Here I will provide a summary of some of the structural features of DNA responsible for its optimal data storage properties. For some readers, this portion of the chapter may seem a bit technical. If that is you, I encourage you to focus on the big picture being communicated. For others, the ensuing discussion won't be technical enough. For these readers, I recommend my book *The Cell's Design*, in which I describe many of the just-right chemical characteristics of DNA that make this molecule uniquely suited to housing genetic information.

The nucleotides that form DNA's double strands are complex molecules. Each one is made of both a phosphate moiety (part of a molecule) and a nucleobase (either adenine, guanine, cytosine, or thymine) joined to deoxyribose, which is a five-carbon sugar. In RNA, ribose (also a five-carbon sugar) replaces deoxyribose and the nucleobase uracil replaces thymine.

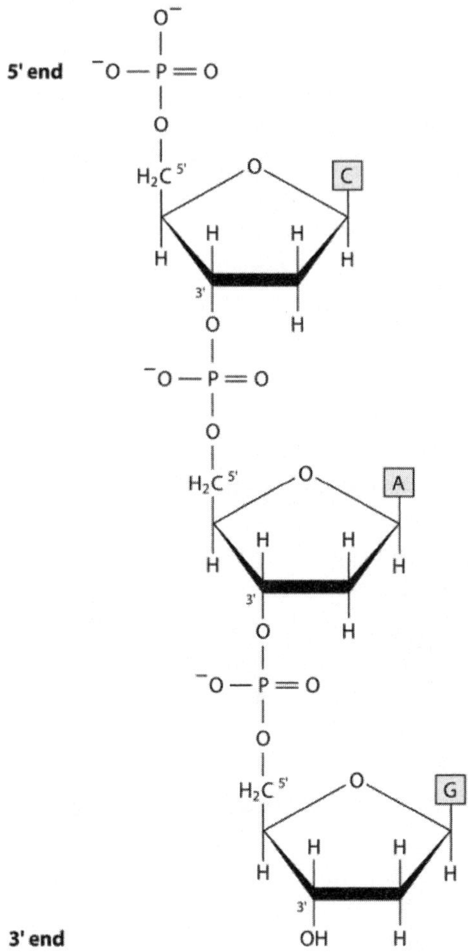

Figure 3.3: DNA Backbone and Side Chains

The backbone of the DNA strand is formed by repeatedly linking the phosphate group of one nucleotide to the deoxyribose unit of another nucleotide.

The backbone of the DNA strand is formed by repeatedly linking the phosphate group of one nucleotide to the deoxyribose unit of another nucleotide. Biochemists call this bond a 5' to 3' phosphodiester linkage. The nucleobases extend as side chains from the sugar-phosphate backbone and serve as interaction points (like ladder rungs) between the two strands.

Scientists have long wondered why the nucleotide subunits of DNA and RNA consist of these molecular components (phosphates, adenine, guanine, cytosine, thymine, uracil, deoxyribose, and ribose), but not others. Myriad sugars and numerous other nucleobases could have conceivably become part of the cell's information storage (DNA) and processing systems (RNA).

Emerging data indicates that the components that make up the nucleotides appear to have been *chosen carefully* with every detail of DNA's structure critically factored into this molecule's information-storage role.

Why Phosphate?

For nearly 35 years, biochemists have understood why phosphates are critical to the structures of DNA and RNA. This chemical group is perfectly suited to form a stable backbone for the DNA molecule. Yet in theory, phosphite, sulfate, or arsenate could have been used instead of phosphate. These compounds are chemical analogs to phosphate.

Phosphates can form bonds with two sugars at the same time (phosphodiester bonds) to bridge two nucleotides, while retaining a negative charge. The negative charge on the phosphate group imparts the DNA backbone with stability that prevents reactive water molecules from cleaving (splitting) it. It also serves as a protein-binding site. Both phosphite and sulfate can form two bonds, but lack a negative charge. And arsenate can't form bonds with organic materials. In other words, an exquisite molecular rationale exists for the inclusion of phosphate in the backbone of DNA (and RNA).

Why a 5' to 3' Phosphodiester Linkage?

The specific nature of the phosphodiester bonds is also optimized. To understand its importance, we need to consider RNA molecules. The phosphodiester linkage that bridges the ribose sugars of RNA could involve the 5' OH of one ribose molecule with either the 2' OH or the 3' OH of the adjacent ribose moiety. In nature, RNA makes use of 5' to 3' bonding exclusively. It turns out that 5' to 3' linkages impart much greater stability to the RNA molecule than 5' to 2' bonds. This means that the 5' to 3' phosphodiester linkage in DNA is a maximally stable bond, providing a rationale for this structural feature of DNA.

Why Deoxyribose and Ribose?

Numerous recent studies indicate why deoxyribose and ribose were selected as the sugar molecules that make up the backbones of DNA and RNA. Deoxyribose and ribose are five-carbon sugars that form five-membered rings.

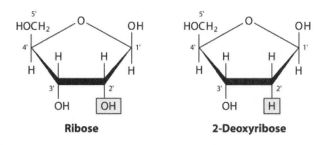

Figure 3.4: Differences between Deoxyribose and Ribose

Deoxyribose and ribose are five-carbon sugars that form five-membered rings. Deoxyribose lacks an OH group at the 2′ position. Ribose possesses a 2′ OH moiety.

Researchers have demonstrated that it is possible to make DNA analogs using a wide range of different sugars that contain four-, five-, and six-carbons that can adopt five- and six-membered rings. But they have also shown that these DNA variants have undesirable properties.

For example, some of these DNA analogs don't form double helices. Others do, but the nucleotide strands interact either too strongly, too weakly, or they display inappropriate selectivity in their associations. Additionally, other studies show that DNA analogs made from sugars that form six-membered rings adopt too many structural conformations. This diversity is unworkable. If DNA assumes multiple conformations, then it becomes extremely difficult for the cell's machinery to replicate, repair, and transcribe DNA properly.

Also, researchers have shown that deoxyribose uniquely provides the necessary space within the DNA backbone to accommodate the large nucleobases. No other sugar fulfills this requirement.

For some time, biochemists have understood why deoxyribose was selected for use in DNA and ribose for RNA. Information storage demands a stable molecule. Incorporation of ribose into DNA would make the molecule inherently unstable. Unlike deoxyribose, ribose possesses a 2' OH group, which can catalyze the cleavage of DNA's sugar-phosphate backbone.

However, ribose is well suited for RNA where some measure of instability is preferable. One of the roles of RNA is to mediate the transfer of information from the nucleotide sequences of DNA to the amino acid sequences of proteins. When the cell needs the protein encoded by a particular gene, the cell's machinery copies mRNA from DNA. Once produced, mRNAs continue to direct the production of proteins at the ribosome until the cell's machinery breaks down the mRNA molecules. Fortunately, mRNA molecules can exist intact for only a brief period in part because of the breakdown of the sugar-phosphate backbone mediated by the 2' OH group. The short lifetime of mRNAs serves the cell well. If mRNAs persisted unduly, then these molecules would direct the production of proteins at the ribosome beyond the point needed by the cell, resulting in the unneeded proteins cluttering the cell's interior.

Why A, G, C, and T?

Like deoxyribose and ribose, the nucleobases adenine, guanine, cytosine, thymine, and uracil found in DNA and RNA appear to be the best possible choices. (The nucleobases are abbreviated A, G, C, T, and U, respectively.) For example, recent research demonstrates that this set of nucleobases displays ideal photophysical properties. The bases found in nature minimize the ultraviolet-induced photophysical damage DNA and RNA experience routinely. In large measure, the damage occurs because the nucleobases absorb electromagnetic wavelengths. Nevertheless, the destructive effects could be far worse. These nucleobases maximally absorb UV radiation at the same wavelengths that are most effectively shielded by ozone. Also, the chemical structures of the nucleobases cause the UV radiation to be efficiently radiated away after absorption, thus limiting the opportunity for damage.

Why T and Not U?

Biochemists also understand why thymine is used in place of uracil in DNA. Uracil is chemically unstable; it undergoes a chemical change (called a deamination) to produce cytosine. Thymine is resistant to that chemical change. Deamination would be problematic for DNA because of its role in information storage. Using thymine instead of uracil staves off this problem. Deamination is not a problem for RNA, which exists transiently inside the cell.

As with DNA's structural features, the selection of A, G, C, and T for building DNA makes chemical sense.

Why Antiparallel Strands?

Biochemists have come to recognize that even the antiparallel arrangement of the nucleotide strands is optimal. Researchers have demonstrated that DNA analogs with a parallel orientation of nucleotide strands can be prepared in the laboratory. By comparing these novel DNA systems with native DNA, it becomes clear that antiparallel alignment of the nucleotide strands leads to greater stability of the DNA double helix found in nature.

DNA Inspires Manmade Tech

Every aspect of DNA's structure plays a critical role in the biomolecule's stability and ability to bind proteins. The exquisite optimization of DNA's structure indicates that it is *not* the outworking of a historically contingent evolutionary process. Instead, its components appear to have been selected carefully and fitted together. If optimization is a hallmark of human designs, then I contend that the molecular logic undergirding DNA's structure and extreme optimization points to a divine creator's handiwork. It also makes it possible for DNA to inspire next-generation technologies.

DNA as a Digital Storage Medium

DNA's data storage capabilities are inspiring nanotechnologists to explore the prospects of using this biomolecule to solve the data storage crisis that confronts humanity.

Forty-four trillion megabytes of digital data exist in the world today. To put this number into context, assuming 10 billion people in the world, each person would have to possess over 6,000 CDs to store all this data. If we continue to generate data at this pace, then by 2040 there will not be enough high-quality silicon to produce ready-access digital data storage devices.

Because DNA approaches the theoretical maximum for digital data storage, one kilogram of DNA can store all the digital data that currently exists. In 2012, as proof of principle, a research team from Harvard University headed by George Church encoded the entire contents of a 54,000-word book into fragments of DNA. In addition, they also encoded 11 jpeg images into the DNA fragments. The researchers also showed that they could read out the information found in the DNA fragments using locater sequences designed into each fragment. These locater sequences function in the same way that page numbers function in a conventional book.

Since then, researchers have encoded computer programs and operating systems into the DNA molecule. Not only are researchers continuing to explore the use of DNA as a digital storage medium, they are also gaining inspiration from DNA's structure and function to design novel man-made polymers with the capabilities of storing digital data.

DNA Computing

As I pointed out in chapter 2, computer scientists and molecular biologists have learned that the cell's machinery that manipulates DNA literally functions like a computer system at its most basic level of operation. The similarity between cellular processes—such as transcription, DNA replication, and DNA repair—and the fundamental operation of computer systems is inspiring an area of nanotechnology called DNA computing.

As mentioned, DNA computers are made up of DNA and the proteins that manipulate this biomolecule inside the cell. These computers are housed in tiny test tubes, yet they are more powerful than the most powerful supercomputer system humans have devised. That power stems largely from the capacity to perform a vast number of parallel computations simultaneously.

Researchers have used DNA computers to solve problems familiar to computer science students that silicon-based supercomputer systems cannot solve, such as the Hamilton path problems and the knight's tour problem.[1] Though promising, DNA computers are still in development. The computations take place rapidly, but researchers have not figured out how to rapidly and efficiently read and write the data housed in DNA sequences.

DNA Wires

In the early 1990s, chemist Jacqueline Barton discovered that DNA can conduct electrical current through its interior along the length of the double helix. Not only that, but DNA can conduct electricity more rapidly and efficiently than "standard" wires. Then, a little over a decade later, Barton and her collaborators showed that charge conductance through the DNA double helix allows the cell's machinery to efficiently detect damage to the double helix that results from chemical or physical insults.

"Surveillance" proteins help detect damage. These proteins migrate along the DNA double helix, occasionally binding to the DNA and sending an electron from an iron-sulfur redox center through the interior of the double helix, which establishes a current through the DNA molecule. Once a surveillance protein loses an electron, it cannot dissociate from the DNA double helix. At this point, other surveillance proteins bound to the DNA pick up the electrons from the interior at their iron-sulfur redox center, then dissociate from the DNA and resume their migration along the double helix. Eventually, the migrating surveillance proteins will bind to the DNA again and dispatch an electron through the molecule's interior.

This process is repeated over and over again. However, if damage has occurred to the DNA molecule, it will distort the double helix and interrupt the flow of electrons through its interior. When this happens, the surveillance proteins remain attached to the DNA, signaling the location of the damage to the DNA repair machinery.

Nanotechnologists have taken note of this specialization and are exploring the use of DNA as nanowires, allowing them to build nanoelectronic devices. Researchers think that DNA nanowires may find specific use in building the next generation of medical diagnostic devices.

DNA Inspires the Case for a Creator

DNA's optimal design not only inspires new technologies, it also inspires the case for a creator. To more fully appreciate why, I would like to turn our attention to William Paley's watchmaker argument for God's existence. As detailed in chapter 2, Paley, an eighteenth-century Anglican natural theologian, posited that just as a watch requires a watchmaker, so too, life requires a creator. In the opening pages of his 1802 book, *Natural Theology*, Paley sets the stage for his famous analogy by comparing a stone to a watch:

> But suppose I had found a watch upon the ground, and it should be inquired how the watch happened to be in that place; I should hardly think of the answer which I had before given [for the stone], that for any thing I knew, the watch might have always been there. . . . When we come to inspect the watch, we perceive (what we could not discover in the stone) that its several parts are framed and put together for a purpose . . . the inference, we think, is inevitable, that the watch must have had a maker: that there must have existed, at some time, and at some place or other, an artificer or artificers who formed it for the purpose which we find it actually to answer; who comprehended its construction, and designed its use.[2]

For Paley, the characteristics of a watch and the complex interaction of its precision parts for time-keeping purposes implied the work of an intelligent designer. Likewise, organisms display a wide range of features characterized by the precise interplay of complex parts for specific purposes. Thus, according to the watchmaker analogy, both watches and organisms display design. Watches are the product of a watchmaker and organisms are the product of a divine creator.

A Watchmaker Prediction

It is straightforward to appreciate how advances in biochemistry have breathed new life into the watchmaker argument. For example, researchers have found computer systems operating within the cell. (Chapter 2 discusses these examples in greater detail.)

In conjunction with my presentation of the revitalized watchmaker argument in my book *The Cell's Design*, I also proposed the watchmaker *prediction*. I contended that many of the cell's molecular systems currently go unrecognized as analogs to human designs because the corresponding technology has yet to be developed. That is, the watchmaker argument may well become stronger in the future and its conclusion more certain as human technology advances.

The possibility that advances in human technology will ultimately mirror existing molecular technology as an integral part of biochemical systems leads to the watchmaker prediction: As human designers develop new technologies, examples of these technologies, which previously went unrecognized, will become evident in the operation of the cell's molecular systems. In other words, if the watchmaker analogy truly serves as evidence for the Creator's existence, then it is reasonable to expect that life's biochemical machinery anticipates human technological advances.

The Converse Watchmaker Argument

A related argument can be dubbed the *converse* watchmaker analogy. If biological designs are the work of a creator, then these systems should be so well designed that they can serve as engineering models and inspire the development of new technologies. In this way, the disciplines of biomimetics and bioinspiration add support for the watchmaker argument. As a scientist, I find the converse watchmaker argument more compelling than Paley's classical analogy. It is remarkable to me that biological designs can inspire engineering efforts. It is even more astounding to think that biomimetics and bioinspiration programs could be so successful *if* biological systems were truly generated by an unguided, historically contingent process.

The Challenge to the Evolutionary Paradigm

As detailed in chapter 2, I have often found that when presented with the watchmaker argument, skeptics will argue that evolutionary processes can serve as the watchmaker. In fact, they regard these processes as the blind watchmaker. However, work in biomimetics and bioinspiration provides a response to the blind watchmaker challenge. To appreciate this challenge, we need to discuss the nature of the evolutionary process.

Evolutionary biologists view biological systems as the outworking of unguided, historically contingent processes that co-opt preexisting designs to cobble together new systems. Once these designs are in place, evolutionary mechanisms can optimize them. Even so, these systems remain, in essence, kludges.

Most evolutionary biologists are quick to emphasize that evolutionary processes and pathways seldom yield perfect designs. Instead, most biological designs are flawed in some way. To be certain, most biologists would concede that natural selection has produced biological designs that are *well adapted*, but they would maintain that biological systems are *not* well designed. Why? Because evolutionary processes do not produce biological systems from scratch. They stem from preexisting systems that are co-opted through a process dubbed exaptation—by the late evolutionary biologist Stephen Jay Gould—and then modified by natural selection to produce new designs. Once formed, these new structures can be fine-tuned and optimized through natural selection to produce well-adapted designs, but not well-designed systems. Biologist Kenneth Miller explains that we should not expect perfection from evolution:

> Evolution . . . does not produce perfection. The fact that every intermediate stage in the development of an organ must confer a selective advantage means that the simplest and most elegant design for an organ cannot always be produced by evolution. In fact, the hallmark of evolution is the modification of pre-existing structures. An evolved organism, in short, should show the tell-tale signs of this modification.[3]

If biological systems are, in effect, kludged together, then why would engineers and technologists turn to them for inspiration? If produced by evolutionary processes—even if these processes operated over the course of millions of years—then biological systems should make unreliable muses. Does it make sense for engineers to rely on biological systems—historically contingent and exapted in their origin—to solve problems and inspire new technologies, much less build an entire subdiscipline of engineering around mimicking biological designs?

Using biological designs to guide engineering efforts seems to be fundamentally incompatible with an evolutionary explanation for life's origin and history. On the other hand, biomimetics and bioinspiration naturally flow out of an intelligent design or creation model approach to biology. Using biological systems to inspire engineering makes better sense if the designs in nature arise from a divine mind.

As a scientist and as a Christian, I find it remarkable how the Old and New Testaments anticipate scientific advancements. When it comes to biomimetics and bioinspiration, Job 12:7–9 immediately comes to mind:

> But ask the animals, and they will teach you, or the birds in the sky, and they will tell you; or speak to the earth, and it will teach you, or let the fish in the sea inform you. Which of all these does not know that the hand of the Lord has done this?

 Resources to Dig Deeper

Fazale Rana, "Insect Biology Advancing Technology," in *God and the World of Insects*, ed. Josh Shoemaker and Gary Braness (Silverton, OR: Lampion Press, 2017), 155–77.

Fazale Rana, *The Cell's Design: How Chemistry Reveals the Creator's Artistry* (Grand Rapids: Baker Books, 2008).

Fazale Rana, "DNA Wired for Design," *The Cell's Design* (blog), *Reasons to Believe*, June 21, 2017, reasons.org/explore/blogs/the-cells-design/read/the-cells-design/2017/06/20/dna-wired-for-design.

Fazale Rana, "DNA: Digitally Designed," *The Cell's Design* (blog), *Reasons to Believe*, May 24, 2017, reasons.org/explore/blogs/the-cells-design/read/the-cells-design/2017/05/24/dna-digitally-designed.

Chapter 4

Why Would a Good God Create Viruses?

Anjeanette "AJ" Roberts, PhD

When people learn I'm a virologist they often ask, "Are viruses alive?" And when they learn that I'm a Christian they often ask, "Why would a *good* God create viruses?" I love to address questions like these and have spent years thinking about viruses and their roles in creation and human sickness, their use as tools in mitigating suffering, and more.

As a Christian who is also a scientist I often use scientific discoveries to help others see how God reveals himself to us in creation. Christian scripture tells us that creation or nature points people to the realization of God's existence.

> The heavens proclaim the glory of God; the skies display his craftsmanship. Day after day they continue to speak; night after night they make him known. They speak without a sound or word; their voice is never heard. Yet their message has gone throughout the earth, and their words to all the world. God has made a home in the heavens for the sun. (Psalm 19:1–4, NLT)

But not just that, nature actually reveals God's power and attributes to us as well. In other words, observing creation, even through scientific discoveries, doesn't just point us to God but shows us what the Creator is like.

> They know the truth about God because he has made it obvious to them. For ever since the world was created, people have seen the earth and sky. Through everything God made, they

clearly see his invisible qualities—his eternal power and divine
nature. So they have no excuse for not knowing God. (Romans
1:19–20, NLT)

So, how might one think about how viruses fit into a model that is scientifically astute and yet shows evidence of creation?

Certainly, some viruses can be very dangerous and even deadly. Historically, viruses were identified because of the diseases they cause (e.g., tobacco
mosaic virus, rabies virus, bird flu, and smallpox). Since many of these viruses
cause severe disease and suffering and even lead to death, then the question,
"Why would a good God create viruses?" is a great question!

Of course, this question assumes that viruses are bad, and it implies that
God is nonexistent, lacking in power, or cruel. In reality, this question reveals a
lack of understanding of viruses and their role in nature.

An Abundance of Viruses

We know of viruses like influenza, herpes, measles (which kills 10 people every
hour[1]), and hemorrhagic fever viruses (like Ebola) that can affect entire populations, causing widespread disease and death, even on a global scale. High
mortality rates can occur—as with the most recent outbreak of Ebola or the
historic 1918 influenza pandemic. But, notable as they are, these viruses are the
rare exceptions.

Recent technological advances and the advent of metagenomics have
changed the way we understand viruses. Scientists now have the capability to
extract DNA (or RNA) from environmental samples and sequence multiple
organisms at once. Through such analyses we now realize that Earth is filled
with a truly vast array and diversity of viruses. Everywhere we find life, we
find viruses. And we find them in overwhelming abundance. A single milliliter
of ocean water or a gram of soil can harbor 10–100 million virus particles or
more.

Viruses outnumber all other living things by a factor of 10 to 1 or even 100
to 1 or more. The vast majority of viruses infect single-celled organisms like
bacteria and archaea. It is estimated that there are 10^{31} viruses on Earth. That's
a one followed by 31 zeroes. That's 10 million times more viruses than stars in
the universe!

That number can be very hard to comprehend or imagine. If we could
weigh all the viruses on Earth together, they would equal the weight of 75 million blue whales.[2] If we could line up all the viruses end to end, they would

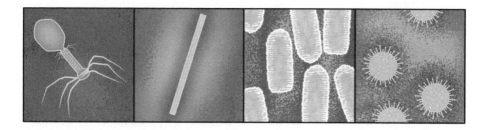

Figure 4: Viruses Show Great Diversity

stretch out 42 million light-years. That's almost 20 round-trips to the Androm-
eda Galaxy. Considering most viruses are on the order of 0.1–0.01 microns, or
one one-thousandth the width of a human hair, that's a lot of viruses!

Yet only an infinitesimal fraction of an infinitesimal fraction of viruses are
associated with human disease, or diseases of any kind. Let me repeat that:
the vast majority of viruses on planet Earth are not associated with disease or
suffering. In fact, they are critical for sustaining balance in Earth's ecological
webs and for providing higher ordered organisms ecological space in which to
thrive.

Are Viruses Alive?
Now, I want to address the question of whether viruses are alive or not because
the answer is important for understanding what may or may not be true about
viral origins.

Viruses are comprised of two basic components: proteins and nucleic acid
(RNA or DNA). Some viruses also have a lipid envelope. They display incred-
ible diversity in size, shape, replication strategies, genomic composition, genomic organization, and in the kinds of cells and animals they infect. Figure
4 depicts some of the broad diversity in virus morphologies (shapes). Viewing
from left to right: we see a virus that infects bacteria, another that infects tobacco plants, then rabies viruses (which infect animals as well as people), and
finally, viruses associated with infantile diarrhea. Estimates suggest that there
are 1–3 million different viruses infecting vertebrates. And one study in bats
indicates that more than 90 percent of viruses infecting mammals have yet to
be identified.

Despite such huge viral diversity, all viruses share one thing in common: they cannot replicate or make more viruses on their own. Living things

consume nutrients, grow and develop, capture and/or produce energy, remove waste, and reproduce either sexually or asexually. Viruses do not. Viruses cannot harvest nutrients from their environment. They absolutely require a living cell host to provide resources, machinery, and energy to produce and assemble viral components into viral progeny or new viruses.

When a virus infects a cell, signals in viral proteins and nucleic acids hijack cellular machinery for viral protein synthesis as viruses depend on cellular metabolic processes and enzymes for provision of nucleobases and amino acids—building blocks for progeny virions. Viruses also depend on intracellular transport systems for many steps in viral replication and assembly. Without living cells, viruses would never replicate.

Replication of viruses is best described by a paper copy machine metaphor. Viruses are like the paper that goes in with information written on it. But the copier provides the ink and paper (the resources), the energy, and the machinery to produce more copies of the paper. Now the metaphor fails a bit because while a photocopied paper is an exact replica, each copy of a virus is not necessarily perfect. Viruses can accrue changes over time as cellular replication machinery may introduce changes (or errors) to viral genetic sequences. Although viruses are not living, they play a critical role in the history of life on Earth and in sustaining biodiversity today.

The Mysterious Origin of Viruses

Now we can address the question of where viruses come from. Like all other viruses, those that infect humans are of unknown etiology. We know that some viruses cross over from animal populations to human populations, like bird and swine flus and rabies. But the ultimate origin of viruses remains unknown.

Rogue Cellular Machinery?

Because viruses are absolutely dependent upon living cells to make more viruses, some scientists think of them as conglomerations of escaped genes from once-living cells. The idea is that particular components somehow escaped functional cells and formed conglomerates that maintained the necessary molecules and information needed for replicating copies of themselves in proper cellular environments. Through subsequent rounds of replication, these viruses likely accrued changes and added various components over time and through continued replication in a variety of organisms.[3]

But this scenario of viral origins is problematic in many ways, not the least of which is that viruses often demonstrate a strict host specificity. They are unable to infect a variety of different kinds of cells or hosts successfully. A restricted host specificity would make it difficult for viruses to pick up a variety of components from vastly different cells. A second complexity is that viruses are radically diverse from one another in replication strategies, not just host specificities. These characteristics suggest that, if true, the escaped gene scenario—where all the tools needed for replication upon entering a host are maintained—has happened countless times in life's history.

Such observations challenge a naturalistic scenario of viral origins. It may be possible, in a world where decay is currently part of the natural order, that *some* viruses originated as defunct cellular machinery gone rogue. Upon reentry into functioning cells these viruses muck-up the normal cellular machinery and lead to disease. Cellular machinery gone rogue? Maybe.

Or Direct Creations?

On the other hand, it is also possible that viruses were *designed* as part of the created order. Consider this: if it were not for viruses, bacteria and other single-celled organisms would rule the planet, sequestering all nutrients and filling all ecological niches, making higher life and the survival of multicellular organisms impossible. Bacteriophage, viruses that infect bacteria and archaea (sometimes called "phage" for short), kill 40–50 percent of the bacteria in Earth's oceans on a daily basis. This bacterial death releases an abundance of biogenic and organic molecules into Earth's biogeochemical cycle and food chain for the survival of other organisms.

Bacteriophage also help keep our planet's ecological niches and our bodies' microbiomes in balance so that we are not overrun by bacteria. If not for a balance between bacterial replication and phage-mediated death, Earth would be a giant ball of bacteria, as bacteria are masters of replication and adaptation. Left unchecked by viruses, rampant bacterial growth would leave no room or food sources for other organisms to survive and thrive. Thankfully, virus replication is controlled by dependence on living cells, which demonstrates a finely tuned system of checks-and-balances between phage and single-celled organisms at the foundation of Earth's biogeochemical cycle.

Viruses that infect and control bacterial populations also contribute to Earth's precipitation cycles. Particles in the atmosphere serve as seeds for nucleation events (clustering) that initiate precipitation. Viruses, along with bacterial proteins that are aerosolized after viral lysis (fracturing of infected bacterial cells), serve as seeds for ice nucleation in the upper atmosphere, thus contributing to precipitation. And, of course, higher life thrives because of

Earth's abundant precipitation cycles.

Many viruses associated with human disease persist in animal reservoirs. These zoonotic viruses may be transferred to human hosts when susceptible individuals come in contact with animals that harbor the virus even in the absence of disease. It is unclear what roles these viruses play in nature before making the jump into human hosts. It's possible that some may exist to regulate animal populations, similar to the way bacteriophage regulate bacterial populations. It is also possible that many may have symbiotic effects in nature and only rarely result in disease when exposure and transmission to susceptible hosts occur from our imperfect management of creation.

In fact, that's what scientists continue to discover: viruses with symbiotic effects. Once unnoticed because no outward sign of disease led to inquiry, these viruses allow plants, insects, and other organisms to survive under otherwise challenging environmental conditions. For example, some viruses allow infected plants survival advantages under drought or cold temperatures that prove detrimental to uninfected plants. Other viral infections render mice and human hosts resistant to yet other subsequent infections. No doubt many more symbiotic relationships will be discovered as we continue to explore the roles of the nearly countless viruses surrounding us.

Viruses as God's Good Creations

In addition to symbiotic effects and critical roles in maintaining ecosystems and biogeochemical and precipitation cycles, viruses can be seen as part of God's creation, providentially given for our use and management. Viruses supply an abundant matrix of untapped genes and delivery systems to address many of the challenges we face in human health and disease and creation care.

Regardless of their origins (or associated diseases), many viruses can and do serve as tools that allow scientists to uncover mysteries of cellular biology, genetically alter organisms, and mitigate disease. Viruses are harnessed for use in gene therapy, cancer therapy, gene editing, vaccine production, and nanomedicine delivery. And these are just a few of the ways scientists have learned to wield viruses for good.

Much of what we know about molecular and cellular biology has been knowledge gained through virus studies. At least 15 Nobel prizes have been awarded for research based on virus-dependent work. For example, viruses were used to discover that DNA (rather than proteins) serves as the substance of heredity, to discover the triplet base codon nature of the genetic code, and to discover RNA splicing and tumor suppressor genes.

Viruses can also be manipulated and engineered to *fight* diseases, including cancers, congenital and genetic diseases, and viral and bacterial diseases. The best-known use of viruses in this respect is probably their use in vaccines such as the polio vaccines. Prior to the advent of the polio vaccines, a 1952 outbreak of polio in the United States led to more than 50,000 infections, over 21,000 cases of paralysis, and over 3,000 deaths. Since the introduction of the inactivated (1955) and oral (1961) polio vaccines, global immunization campaigns have dropped the number of cases from over 350,000 cases per year in 1988, to less than 500 cases per year in 2013. According to the latest World Health Organization targets, the year 2018 could see the complete eradication of infectious poliovirus.[4]

Viruses are now being used to fight cancers directly and as shuttles to deliver gene-editing molecules to combat cancers such as sarcoma, melanoma, and myeloma. Gene editing, using viruses as delivery mechanisms, may one day eliminate other congenital and genetic diseases as well as chronic infectious diseases such as HIV.

The potential use of viruses to help fight human disease and steward creation through such things as enhancing agricultural crops (making them more resistant to disease, pestilence, or drought or enhancing their nutritional or medicinal effects) is immense and exciting. Viruses may prove to be the *best molecular tool for human use ever known*. Viruses may also be the next best weapon to fight multi-drug resistant bacteria too!

Multi-drug resistant bacteria are still susceptible to bacteriophage lysis. Identifying and isolating the appropriate phage and determining ways to keep the phage lytic will allow us to keep some of the most pathogenic bacteria in check when antibiotics continue to fail.

Concluding Thoughts

Although a few viruses are remarkably bad, we dare not put all viruses in that category. In fact, life as we know it would not be possible, and our thriving as human beings and caretakers of creation would be impossible without the vast array of viruses that fill the planet.

It is clear that some viruses were certainly part of the created order since the vast majority of life and biodiversity on Earth would not be possible without bacteriophage. Apart from direct creation, some small subset of viruses may originate through decay of natural systems, as cellular cast-offs or escape genes. Some may lead to disease primarily through our ignorance and mismanagement of creation. Still, others seem to be providentially supplied by a good creator for our discovery, harvest, and transformation in mitigating disease and suffering and even improving creation care. Whether viruses are individually created or occasional cast-offs, creation's design certainly necessitates a vast storehouse of diverse viruses for keeping life well regulated, whether in the human gut or the global biogeochemical cycles.

With such an abundance of still-unknown viruses, we have so much more to discover—and so many reasons to marvel at God's amazing creation and providence. Thanks be to God!

 ## Resources to Dig Deeper

Anjeanette Roberts, *Why Would a Good God Create Viruses?* (Covina, CA: Reasons to Believe, 2017), DVD.

Anjeanette Roberts, "Celebrating 3.8 Billion Years of Bacteriophage," *Today's New Reason to Believe* (blog), *Reasons to Believe*, October 22, 2015, reasons.org/explore/publications/tnrtb/read/tnrtb/2015/10/23/celebrating-3.8-billion-years-of-bacteriophage.

Anjeanette Roberts, "More Viruses Than Stars? No Way!," *Theorems & Theology* (blog), *Reasons to Believe*, September 22, 2016, reasons.org/explore/blogs/theorems-theory/read/theorems-theory/2016/09/22/more-viruses-than-stars-no-way!.

Anjeanette Roberts, "Vaccine Safety and Loving Our Neighbors," *Today's New Reason to Believe* (blog), *Reasons to Believe*, October 15, 2015, reasons.org/explore/blogs/todays-new-reason-to-believe/read/tnrtb/2015/10/20/vaccine-safety-and-loving-our-neighbors.

Hugh Ross, "Another Reason to Thank God for Viruses," *Today's New Reason to Believe* (blog), *Reasons to Believe*, October 31, 2016, reasons.org/explore/blogs/todays-new-reason-to-believe/read/todays-new-reason-to-believe/2016/10/31/another-reason-to-thank-god-for-viruses.

Hugh Ross, "More Reasons to Thank God for Viruses," *Today's New Reason to Believe* (blog), *Reasons to Believe*, May 15, 2016, reasons.org/explore/blogs/to-days-new-reason-to-believe/read/todays-new-reason-to-believe/2017/05/15/more-reasons-to-thank-god-for-viruses.

Fazale Rana, "Viruses and God's Providence," *Today's New Reason to Believe* (blog), *Reasons to Believe*, June 11, 2009, reasons.org/explore/publications/tnrtb/read/tnrtb/2009/06/11/viruses-and-god's-providence.

Fazale Rana, "Viruses and God's Providence Revisited," *Today's New Reason to Believe* (blog), *Reasons to Believe*, November 26, 2009, reasons.org/explore/publications/tnrtb/read/tnrtb/2009/11/26/viruses-and-god's-providence-re-visited.

Chapter 5

Unequivocating Evolution

Anjeanette "AJ" Roberts, PhD

Perhaps you have heard people claim that there is more evidence for evolution than there is that Earth revolves around the Sun. I have been asked if I thought this statement was true. Well, to answer, I would have to turn to a common response I learned while living in Russia. I frequently heard Russians reply to thought-provoking questions with a phrase that translates to "it depends."

So, the answer to the claim regarding evolution is it depends on what you mean by the word *evolution*.

People often equivocate the word *evolution*. Equivocation is a process that hinges on one word having multiple meanings. It involves using a word in a context where the meaning is glossed over in order to make a faulty assertion seem more defensible. By equivocating you're assuming one meaning, but actually using the word in a different context.

This often happens when people discuss evolution. A statement like "There's more evidence for evolution than that Earth revolves around the Sun" may or may not be true depending on what one means by "evolution." So, we're going to *un*equivocate the word *evolution*.

I find it helpful to understand that *evolution* is used to describe five categories of naturalistic processes (chemical evolution, microevolution, microbial evolution, speciation, and macroevolution), each dependent on different underlying mechanisms. Some people also use the term simultaneously to refer to all *naturalistic* processes accounting for the history and diversity of life on Earth—which, as we will see, is classic equivocation.

Chemical Evolution

Also known as abiogenesis, chemical evolution refers to the process of generating life from nonlife. It's the proposed mechanism for the naturalistic explanation for the origin of life (OOL). Chemical evolution involves the synthesis of biogenic molecules from simple molecules and the generation of simple, self-replicating cells or protocells. This is what chemical evolution entails, but it faces some difficult hurdles as far as scientific evidence is concerned. Here I'll address four significant difficulties: (1) challenges to prebiotic chemistry, (2) the chiral nature of biomolecules, (3) system-level information, and (4) the early appearance of life on Earth.

Prebiotic Chemistry

Synthesis of various prebiotic molecules and biomolecules requires various chemical environments. Even the simplest cell needs many biomolecules, including nucleic acids, proteins, carbohydrates, and fatty acids. It's true that early Earth would have had the inorganic precursors needed to build prebiotic molecules; nevertheless, synthesizing those molecules and larger bio-macro-molecules via abiotic (nonliving) pathways presents a major challenge.

All biomolecules have special chemical requirements for synthesis—temperature, pH, presence of specific compounds in solution, solvent type, presence or absence of oxygen, reaction kinetics, etc. Requirements for synthesis of some biomolecules differ radically from the conditions for other prebiotic molecules and cellular components. In fact, the conditions for synthesizing some components are destructive for other compounds. So, the first hurdle for abiogenesis is the incompatibility of the chemistries needed for the synthesis of the broad range of necessary cellular components.

Furthermore, many abiotic chemical reactions also produce contaminating compounds that make the synthesis of biopolymers of nucleotides (in nucleic acids) and amino acids (in proteins) of biologically functional significance very challenging. It is true that many biomolecules can be synthesized from prebiotic compounds through defined and sometimes even common pathways. However, the generation of—not to mention the need for sequestering and concentrating—biologically relevant compounds via unguided abiotic processes under early Earth conditions is extremely unlikely.

Homochirality

The second hurdle is the challenge of homochirality. In a naturalistic explanation of the OOL the nucleic acids (in RNA and DNA) and amino acids (in proteins), which all share a characteristic of homochirality, must be accounted for.

Chirality refers to the orientation of a molecule. It is sometimes called the "handedness" of a molecule. If you look at your hands, you will see that they are mirror images of one another. Although both have a palm, a thumb, and four fingers you cannot superimpose one on the other because their orientation (or configuration) is one of mirror opposites. The same is true for the configuration of some biogenic molecules.

It is true for the sugars deoxyribose (in DNA) and ribose (in RNA) and for 19 of the 20 canonical biological amino acids. (Glycine is an achiral exception.) All sugars in biological organisms have a single orientation (right-handedness). Almost all chiral amino acids in biological organisms have a single orientation (left-handedness).

The problem is that most naturally occurring reactions do not produce homochiral (same-handed) solutions of right-handed sugars or left-handed amino acids. Most natural (and laboratory) syntheses produce a mixed, racemic solution of sugars or amino acids of roughly 50 percent left- and 50 percent right-handed orientations. Yet in stark contrast, biological processes (those inside the cell) produce only right-handed sugars and left-handed amino acids—perfect building blocks for RNAs, DNAs, and proteins. The homochirality of biological synthesis allows DNA, RNA, and protein synthesis to proceed without the complication of steric inhibition, chain termination, and misfolding that would result if polymerization occurred, drawing from racemic mixtures of nucleic or amino acids, like those produced in *ex vivo* (outside of the organism) reactions.

Almost all life has only D-sugars and L-amino acids in their nucleic acids and proteins. Yet there are no known naturally occurring mechanisms for generating, selecting, and stably maintaining homochirality for either sugars or amino acids under plausible prebiotic conditions or at feasible concentrations.[1]

System-Level Information

A third hurdle in a naturalistic account for the OOL is the need to account for the presence of information in the primary sequence of DNA in an organism's genome. DNA is the blueprint within the cell. It encodes, at a molecular level via RNA intermediates, the information needed for gene expression, regulation, and protein synthesis. Naturalistic mechanisms cannot yet provide a source of that information.

It can be argued that the existence of information in DNA requires the existence of an intelligent programmer and that this concept provides evidence of a creator. (Fazale Rana makes this case for a creator in greater detail in chapters 2 and 3.) Some people will take this argument for creation a step further by claiming that the information in DNA is the most critical information to account for in an OOL scenario. It is true that, if abiogenesis is to stand, then there needs to be a plausible explanation for the generation of such complex information from unguided, non-teleological naturalistic properties. As of today, proponents of abiogenesis have yet to produce that explanation. However, the information in DNA is not, in fact, the most complex information problem in the cell or in organisms.

The information required at a cellular, or system, level is far more intricate than just the primary nucleic acid sequences that code for cellular components and gene regulation. A cell requires information on how to sequester, orient, and assemble machinery involved in metabolic processes, protein trafficking, and energy utilization and acquisition. And it needs information to coordinate the proper relationship and interaction of the various subcellular systems. These processes, subsystems, and various components are integrated and interdependent in complex and finely orchestrated fashions. If this were not so, then life at the cellular level would be impossible.

For an analogy, imagine building an automobile from the ground up. You would need all the necessary parts of a car (wheels, chassis, engine, etc.), which implies the ability to produce (and refine, in the case of gasoline) all those components. And yet parts alone are not enough to build an automobile. It would be impossible to construct the vehicle without information on how all the parts are meant to fit together so that the end product functions properly. An automobile requires independent production of gasoline and proper assembly of the metal, plastic, and rubber parts in proper orientation and number to allow for controlled combustion, cooling and exhaust mechanisms, and locomotion. Temporal controls are also necessary—for example, you would never add gasoline before assembling the other parts. Without the assembly of the functioning complex the information on how to produce the component pieces does not result in a functioning automobile. Similarly, the information in DNA, which produces the components of a cell, marks only one level of relatively simple information. By comparison, higher order, system-level information accounts for complex cell structures and orchestrated functional interactions, as well as energy acquisition and production and recycling of its own component pieces.

Really, the automobile analogy is way too simple when considering the complexity of living organisms. A more relevant analogy is to consider the information needed for every moving piece and all the interactions of all the various components in a city such as Istanbul in order to mirror the magnitude of complexity of the information in human cells.

Life's Appearance on Earth

The fourth hurdle facing chemical evolution is life's very early appearance—perhaps as early as 4.1 billion years ago (BYA)—a date that predates the rock formations in Earth's crust. Scientists have discovered zircon crystals trapped in ancient rock formations that date to 4.1 BYA and that contain a form of carbon associated with organic or biological sources. This assertion is contentious, but even if we reject this date, additional evidence suggests that carbonate-containing sedimentary mounds (stromatolites) built by secretion of cyanobacteria communities date life's origins to earlier than 3.7 BYA.

Extreme environments would have been present on early Earth at 4.1 BYA, and we know today that extremophiles can live in extraordinary high levels of heat, pressure, salinity, and radioactivity and in extremely low levels of light and oxygen. Since we have access to modern extremophiles, we know that life can exist in very hostile environments. Although the existence of life in extreme environments is possible, it is much less likely that abiotic processes could generate life under such harsh conditions.

Life via Panspermia

The lack of evidence for a plausible naturalistic explanation of life's origins is so challenging that many scientists, clinging to naturalistic paradigms, embrace the theory of panspermia. This is the theory that life, or at least the biogenic molecules necessary for life, originated someplace else in the universe. These seeds of life were then transported, either naturally or intentionally, to Earth.

Yet, panspermia simply displaces chemical evolution's hurdles to some other imagined, unknown site in the universe. The problems of life's origins remain the same anywhere in the universe: incompatible chemistries for producing prebiotic molecules and bio-macromolecules, homochirality of sugars and amino acids in biological compounds, system-level information, and early appearance of complex and diverse life.

Some people point out that many prebiotic compounds and biomolecules may be produced under interstellar space conditions and delivered to Earth by meteorites. Even so, relative concentrations and stable sequestration of specific compounds, in the absence of interfering compounds, in a life-conducive chemical environment for the various building blocks to coalesce in a just-so fashion necessary to produce self-replicating cells under early Earth conditions is an extremely high hurdle to clear. So, chemical evolution as a naturalistic explanation for the OOL is not a logical conclusion drawn from current scientific evidence.

Microevolution

Microevolution is the process of accruing unguided mutations in DNA sequences. Ultimately, such mutations have either a neutral, positive, or negative effect on an organism's ability to survive and reproduce.

Naturalistic processes and competition will select against deleterious mutations. If an organism loses function or becomes unfit, and if it's not as strong a competitor, then deleterious mutations are going to be selected against. Neutral mutations are obviously going to allow the organism to continue to reproduce and survive as before. And any gain of fitness that an organism might experience as the result of a positive mutation is going to be environmentally specific. It's only a gain of fitness for the particular environment in which the selection has taken place.

What are the mechanisms and characteristics of microevolution? They are really just two-fold: unguided mutations and natural selection (hallmarks of Darwinian and neo-Darwinian evolution). The mutations occur, in part, due to different types of stress. Stress can occur, for example, via UV and other forms of radiation or heat or physiological responses to chemicals or hormones. And as a result, the DNA can become damaged, even break. Fortunately, DNA repair mechanisms exist within the cell. Repair mechanisms rejoin broken ends of DNA or remove altered bases—often resulting in mutations at the site of repair. Mutations occur via loss of nucleotides or through the introduction of other nucleic acids at damaged and repaired sites.

Unguided mutations in the nucleic acid sequence can also occur during DNA replication due to infidelity of the polymerase protein as it copies the nucleic acid sequence. Although DNA polymerases have the ability to correct mistakes as they replicate DNA, the polymerase is not 100 percent efficient in replication, as noted by its error rate of about 1 in 10 million base pairs. Thus, breaks in DNA can introduce mutations, repair of DNA can introduce mutations, and replication of the DNA can introduce mutations.

The main point is that in the processes of microevolution mutations are unguided and will have a deleterious, neutral, or beneficial effect as selected through natural pressures. This means that when a mutation occurs, if it is a mutation that allows the organism to survive and thrive in a given environment, then that organism will survive and thrive *and* replicate. If, on the other hand, it is a deleterious mutation within a given environment, then the mutated organism will not survive nor thrive. In microevolution, natural environmental pressures are driving or constraining molecular adaptations over multiple reproductive cycles.

It's obvious that natural selection is non-teleological, meaning it does not have a goal. Natural selection is blind to ultimate purposes. It cannot foresee which mutations might one day provide a fitness advantage in a different environment or in a more complex organism. This is a very important element of Darwinian evolution—it's survival of the fittest. This doesn't mean that an organism is somehow becoming more fit for the future or that it is becoming more fit in a self-directed manner. It is simply that those lacking fitness are being selected against. They're neither surviving nor passing on their genes.

I have found the blindness of natural selection to be one of the biggest confusions for people talking about evolution, specifically about cellular and molecular biological processes. They tend to endow organisms with a teleology of their own. The molecules or organisms are self-directing toward some explicit goal in the present or future. You can find this idea in books like Richard Dawkins's *The Selfish Gene*. He endows the gene with an intention to survive and propagate. At best, that is a philosophical statement through and through. At worst, it is utterly nonsensical. It is not scientifically based. In fact, the notion of intentional natural selection is counterintuitive to what we know to be true about how scientific mechanisms and processes work. But cells and organisms are so richly endowed with complexity and adaptive capacities that it is hard to describe such layers of complexity without resorting to intentional, creative language.

What microevolution actually does is allow organisms to adapt to changing environments. It allows optimization to particular environmental situations or ecological niches of a subset of the population and, through neutral mutations and genetic drift, spread of microevolutionary changes throughout whole populations.

Microbial Evolution
Microbial evolution refers to the rapid and adaptive reproduction of unicellular organisms—such as bacteria, archaea, simple eukaryotes, yeast, etc.—in changing environments via selection of beneficial microevolutionary mutations and promiscuous gene swapping.

Many bacteria, as well as single-celled eukaryotes, can exchange genetic information. Bacteria do so three different ways. First, they can do it through conjugation, where bacteria come in physical contact with one another and one bacterium transfers genetic material to another bacterium. Second, they can exchange genetic information via transduction, which is vector-mediated. Viruses that infect bacteria can transfer nucleic acid (RNA or DNA) upon infection. So, following viral infection, bacteria have picked up additional genetic information. Plus, any progeny virions can pick up genetic information from the infected bacteria and transfer it to additional bacteria upon subsequent infections.

The third way for exchanging genetic information is through transformation (or transfection). When bacteria undergo lysis, their genetic material is released into the environment and the other bacteria can pick up DNA from the environment via transformation. Scientists frequently use this method in the lab when cloning or producing large amounts of DNA by transforming plasmids (circular DNA) into competent bacteria via electroporation or heat shock. All of these methods of genetic exchange are types of horizontal gene transfer, something that happens in unicellular organisms on an ongoing basis. It is a definite driving force in microbial evolution.

Microevolutionary processes also help account for changes in unicellular organisms that result in microbial evolution. As previously mentioned, these microevolutionary mutations are unguided, non-teleological, and can be deleterious, neutral, or beneficial. For single-celled organisms any change in the genetic components (chromosome or plasmids) of one individual organism has subsequent potential to change the entire population in a very rapid manner because every progeny from that one cellular organism now carries the same mutations.

Again, natural selection is acting on single-celled organisms. Those that lose fitness will be selected against, those that haven't had a change in fitness will be maintained, and those that make a positive gain in fitness will thrive. However, any positive gain will be for the particular environment in which the natural selection occurs, not for every subsequent environment. Microbial evolution, like microevolution, allows adaptation to changing environments and optimization to specific ecological niches.

Speciation

Evolution isn't the only word that needs to be unequivocated. Another word that people frequently equivocate when discussing evolution is *species*. This equivocation actually has a recognized name: the "species problem." The species problem results from a wide range of approaches to defining how species are identified and how species function in nature. Each approach is known as a species concept. The number and types of species concepts that exist are constantly changing, but there are at least 26 recognized species concepts today. That's phenomenal!

So, when talking about evolution and the process of speciation we must ask, "What do we mean by species?" Because unless we can clarify that, we can't communicate. For example, we know *species* is a taxonomic level (species, genus, family, order, class, phyla, kingdom), but even so, our intended meaning of *species* is dependent upon which type of organism we are talking about. Thus, when we talk about speciation it is critical that we realize that equivocation might be involved.

Speciation refers to the process in which a given species becomes genetically, phenotypically, and behaviorally distinct, typically due to geographical isolation, resulting in reproductively independent populations. Speciation can also be a radiation event where multiple species result from changes to a single starting species due to variable environmental pressures in a series of isolated geographical and ecological niches. Each resultant species will be genetically, phenotypically, and behaviorally distinct from the starting species and from one another.

In isolation, organisms undergo different types of environmental stresses and pressures that affect the population at a microevolutionary level and at a genetic-drift level. These variable stresses and environmental pressures can also result in epigenetic changes that can affect a species' phenotype and behavior and lead to the isolation of independently reproducing groups. These new groups may become so distinct that they no longer reproduce cross-species; that is, they do not reproduce with the originating species or with the other species radiating from the same event. Two examples of speciation are Darwin's finches and North American canids.

Finches
During his voyages on the HMS *Beagle*, Charles Darwin discovered 15 or 16 different types of finches on the Galápagos Islands. He himself was unaware that the birds he characterized were all finches, but when he took his data back to England others realized he had discovered an array of different types of finches. Thickness of the beaks was one of the distinguishing features. In much more recent studies, scientists have examined environmental pressures that result in

changes to beak morphology. The type of environment in which these finches live and how and where they scavenge for food determines beak length, width, and thickness. Recent observations indicate that morphology changes occur in an oscillating fashion.[2] In dry climates beaks widen and thicken; in wet climates beaks become thin and narrow.

This suggests that distinction of various species results, in part, from a sort of phenotypic plasticity that is adaptive to varying environmental changes. In other words, many adaptive changes are not progressions toward something utterly new, or something that is unidirectional. Rather, they indicate a range of variation that manifests as oscillating changes. For finches, as the environment changes so their beaks change to suit the environment. It's a fluid situation of some characteristics that are environmentally driven. In this respect it is important to note that natural selection is not necessarily unidirectional toward some progressive end. It is also not driving a population from one taxonomic classification to another that distinguishes anything more than a variation of a similar kind.

All of Darwin's finches were finches. Darwin did not see any finches that had evolved into any other type of bird, even though the Galápagos Islands support waterfowl, hawks, and other types of birds. Darwin only observed variations within a single kind of bird—a finch. This observation is also true for Stephen Jay Gould, an evolutionary biologist who studied radiations of snails in island environments. He and others observed radiation events due to isolation of snails in different environments on different islands and in different portions of the same island. The snails acquired characteristics that allowed them to thrive in the ecological niches they inhabited. But, again, one didn't see snails giving rise to different types of organisms—only other snails. Natural selection on genetic variations resulted in adaptive diversification within snails.

Wolves

Most recently, genomic analyses indicate that some North American wolves seem to be hybrids of various canids. For example, red wolves and eastern wolves are geographically and phenotypically distinct and are protected as endangered species, however, both species appear to be genetic hybrids of coyotes and gray wolves, a recent discovery and distinction that might threaten their protected status. Much like selective breeding that has resulted in a wide range of dog breeds, wolves and coyotes seem to be the result of variations over time within an ongoing species-radiation event. No doubt populations are isolated now due to phenotypic and behavioral changes, but possibly not genetically isolated from potential crossbreeding.

New Wasps?

These types of speciation events can occur in ecologically linked, co-adapting species too. A 2015 *Science News* report on a recent study touted the evolution of three new wasp species. In reality, the original study doesn't show that at all. What the researchers observed was a change in plants that affected flies that fed on the plants and, thus, wasps that fed on the flies. Environmental changes triggered mutations in the existing plants in a given ecological niche. As a result of these changes, various flies altered their feeding behaviors. Researchers noted significant behavioral changes, some other phenotypic changes, and some genetic changes in wasps as a result of the changes to the flies.

But despite the changes, the researchers started with three species of wasps and ended with three species of wasps that were, to a certain extent, genetically, phenotypically, and behaviorally altered. The researchers did not examine whether the wasps were reproductively isolated following these changes. What this type of speciation event indicates is that environmental changes can drive various species—plants, flies, and wasps—to co-adapt. This research shows a connection of species within an ecological web, but it has no significance for evolution of a particular species at one taxonomical level to a species of a different taxonomical classification. And as the North American canid study shows, even if you called the new species something entirely different (wolf or coyote or dog), it does not mean that one kind of canid has given rise to anything other than another kind of canid.

Finally, consider speciation in the context of what we believe as Christians, that there was a primordial human pair (Adam and Eve), that the Torah says God created male and female in his image. And if you believe the scientific data that traces mitochondrial Eve to roughly 150,000 years ago and Y-chromosomal Adam to about the same time frame, plus or minus the range of error, then you believe that God created man and woman about 150,000 years ago as a primordial pair. Yet, if you look around today you see immense diversity in the human population. Consider the differences between the major races and ethnicities. Compare some of the island groups in Australia to Asian and Middle Eastern or European or Native American peoples. Consider dwarfs or extremely tall people. Regardless of our extreme diversity we are all human. We are all *Homo sapiens sapiens*.

Macroevolution

The fifth and final category of evolution is macroevolution. This is one area where the term *evolution* is most notably equivocated. What I mean by macroevolution is large-scale functional and structural changes of populations through time, all at or above the species level. Macroevolution refers to a series of naturalistic processes, occurring over long stretches of time, that account for all of life's history, forms, and complexity and that result from descent with modification under pressures of natural selection, acting upon unguided (chance) changes in population genetics (genetic drift), in a contingent and non-teleological manner.

It is supposed that macroevolution entails multiple diverse mechanisms. Successful macroevolutionary changes require large changes in DNA at the cellular level. The process of genome duplication (reproduction of genetic material) is one mechanism capable of generating large amounts of DNA. This provides more genetic material to play with (accruing neutral changes) while maintaining the necessary genetic components for normal function. However, in our current experience, genome duplication is not safe for higher organisms. When we see it occur in multicellular animals today it is typically associated with cancerous cells.

Translocation (jumping genes) is a mechanism where certain elements of DNA have the ability to replicate and move to a new location in a different chromosome or to a different part of the genome. Frequently, translocation in the human genome is linked with disease. So again, these changes are not particularly healthy in our modern observations. Most of these types of mutations would be considered deleterious.

Horizontal gene transfer in multicellular organisms is very dissimilar to the type of horizontal gene transfer that occurs in unicellular organisms. In unicellular life-forms, horizontal gene transfer can occur through viral vectors; some may even be retroviral vectors like those associated with endogenous retrovirus elements found in the genomes of many different animals. Yet when horizontal gene transfer occurs in multicellular, sexually reproducing organisms, a simple transfer of genetic material from a virus to the somatic cell will not be passed on to subsequent generations. For such mutations to have a generational or a population effect, the change must affect the gametes (either the egg or sperm) or their respective gametic precursor cells.

Co-option

Co-option is the process by which one organism becomes dependent on the biological functions provided by another organism. It also refers to the process by which a structure or system with an original function is added to or changes to produce a new function. At an organismic level co-option involves bacteria that provide vital functions for the organisms in which they live. An extreme example of co-option is symbiogenesis or endosymbiosis. This is a mechanism by which naturalists envision the production of the first eukaryotic cell from prokaryotic or protocell precursors.

Prokaryotic cells lack intercellular organelles. Eukaryotic cells are much more complex with their membrane-bound nuclei, endoplasmic reticulum, Golgi apparatus, and other organelles such as mitochondria. Symbiogenesis is employed as an explanatory mechanism where one relatively simplistic prokaryotic cell co-opts another prokaryotic or protocell via phagocytosis or some type of internalization. The result is two previously independent precursors now functioning as a more complex eukaryotic-like cell. Naturalists propose co-option of an entire unicellular organism or protocell to account for the increased complexity in eukaryotic cells compared to prokaryotic or protocell precursors. This explanation may seem plausible for the origin of mitochondria, cytoplasts, or other organelles. However, it offers no assistance in explaining the origination of other intracellular, membrane-bound compartments such as the nucleus, the endoplasmic reticulum, or the Golgi apparatus.

Although naturalists have appealed to many hypotheses, no plausible account has yet to rationally and reasonably describe the muddy middle layer of mechanism. No credible mechanism or explanation for generating true novelty has yet been postulated. No account can be given for the rapid fossil record appearance of most known phyla (extinct and extant) that occurred ~540 million years ago. No true transitional species has ever been identified in the fossil record or through phylogenetic analyses. No genetic map exists showing a clear pathway from one order (or higher) to another. Genomic data supports modular components compatible with a model of common design as well as or better than a model entailing neutral theory, natural selection, and common descent.

Michael Denton asserts that "the [Darwinian theory] is *insufficient* (emphasis added); it does not give a credible and comprehensive explanation of how the pattern of life on earth emerged. It is *incomplete* (emphasis added) and does not give an account of all biological phenomena."[3]

It is not just theists and proponents of intelligent design who challenge macroevolutionary failures, but many committed naturalists also challenge a Darwinian paradigm of gradual accrual of change over time by natural selection. It lacks supporting evidence and even hinders scientific advancement and discovery by forcing data interpretation into a common descent narrative.

Responding to Naturalists

As we've covered in brief, scientific evidence supports microevolution, microbial evolution, and speciation. However, the scientific evidence to date for chemical evolution (abiogenesis) or macroevolution is far less convincing. So, if someone tries to equivocate and make the statement that there is more evidence for evolution than there is that Earth revolves around the Sun, hopefully you will feel confident in challenging their statement.

Nevertheless, for many committed naturalists even a dearth of evidence for their view will not persuade them to reconsider their position. What then do we do with the evidence? Each of us knowingly or unknowingly interprets the data in a way that fits into our view of reality. I believe that the scientific data overwhelmingly points to life-forms replete—even at the simplest level—with highly orchestrated processes requiring system-level information that entails molecular mechanisms that allow adaptation, ensuring survival of diverse species that exist for prolonged periods of stasis without major changes in kinds.

As a scientist, I would argue that there is more evidence for molecular-based adaptation of highly complex and wildly diverse organisms than there is that Earth revolves around the Sun. And I believe that this evidence strongly supports a view of progressive creationism and a common design model. God created life, over long epochs of time, according to specific kinds. And as any good engineer would do, God endowed his creatures with the ability to adapt to challenging and changing environments for their continued survival and thriving. This endowment entails molecular plasticity and a range of possible phenotypes for a given population of organisms. Progressive creationism is a reasonable, rational conclusion, concordant with the data, accounting for the diversity and early appearance of complex life on Earth, the Cambrian explosion, adaptive higher-order organisms, and human exceptionalism. Progressive creationism also accounts for the fine-tuning and intelligibility of the universe.

As one first-century follower of Jesus puts it, "For ever since the world was created, people have seen the earth and sky. Through everything God made, they can clearly see his invisible qualities—his eternal power and divine nature. So they have no excuse for not knowing God."[4]

In the twenty-first century, philosopher and former atheist Antony Flew, who converted to theism before his death, echoes this biblical observation in his book *There Is a God: How the World's Most Notorious Atheist Changed His Mind*:

> Science spotlights three dimensions of nature that point to God. The first is the fact that nature obeys laws. The second is the dimension of life, of intelligently organized and purpose-driven beings, which arose from matter. The third is the very existence of nature. But it is not science alone that guided me. I have also been helped by a renewed study of the classical philosophical arguments. . . . We have all the evidence we need in our immediate experience and that only a deliberate refusal to "look" is responsible for atheism of any variety.[5]

In extreme contrast, Francis Crick, co-discoverer of the DNA double helix, writes in *What Mad Pursuit*, "Biologists must constantly keep in mind that what they see was not designed, but rather evolved."[6] Why does Crick insist such a reminder is necessary? Because design is apparent everywhere one looks! In order to remain committed like Crick and other neo-Darwinists to a naturalistic philosophy—rather than to the scientific evidence—one must refuse to look and constantly remind oneself of naturalism's mantra of evolution. A mantra that fails to account for life's origin, the rapid and early appearance of diverse and complex life, and species' abilities to adapt to changing environments while maintaining stasis in kind.

In contrast to this restrictive commitment to naturalistic explanations, a Christian or theistic paradigm is actually better for science. According to a Christian understanding of creation, God, and nature, we must observe the world in order to know what it is like. Natural laws allow reproducible regularities and nature itself is a reliable revelation of God the Creator. The Scriptures also tell us that truth can be sought and obtained. If we seek we will find when we seek with all of our heart. This is a promise of Jesus, recorded in the gospel.

The Scriptures, like Psalm 104 and Romans 1, assure us that God has in fact created us for inquiry and discovery and that God wants to be known, having revealed himself in nature and in Scripture. So those who seek and do not refuse to look at the evidence will surely find.

Thanks be to God!

Resources to Dig Deeper

Anjeanette Roberts, "What Exactly Is Novelty in Evolution?" *Theorems & Theology* (blog), *Reasons to Believe*, December 1, 2016, reasons.org/explore/blogs/theorems-theory/read/theorems-theory/2016/12/01/what-exactly-is-novelty-in-evolution.

Anjeanette Roberts, "Mutations—How They Work and Which Worldview They Favor," *Theorems & Theology* (blog), *Reasons to Believe*, November 27, 2017, reasons.org/explore/blogs/theorems-theory/read/theorems-theory/2017/11/27/mutations-how-they-work-and-which-worldview-they-favor.

Anjeanette Roberts. "What Species Problem?" *Theorems & Theology* (blog), *Reasons to Believe*, October 6, 2016, reasons.org/explore/blogs/theorems-theory/read/theorems-theory/2016/10/06/what-species-problem.

Hugh Ross, *Improbable Planet: How Earth Became Humanity's Home* (Grand Rapids: Baker Books, 2016).

Fazale Rana, "Evolutionary Paradigm Lacks Explanation for Origin of Mitochondria and Eukaryotic Cells," *The Cell's Design* (blog), *Reasons to Believe*, October 3, 2017, reasons.org/explore/blogs/the-cells-design/read/the-cells-design/2017/10/03/evolutionary-paradigm-lacks-explanation-for-origin-of-mitochondria-and-eukaryotic-cells.

Fazale Rana, "Science News Flash: 3.7-Billion-Year-Old Fossils Perplex Origin-of-Life Researchers," *The Cell's Design* (blog), *Reasons to Believe*, September 7, 2016, reasons.org/explore/blogs/the-cells-design/read/the-cells-design/2016/09/07/science-news-flash-3.7-billion-year-old-fossils-perplex-origin-of-life-researchers.

Chapter 6

Human Origins:
Common Design or Common Descent?

Fazale R. Rana, PhD

In the West, one of the most contentious aspects of the creation-evolution controversy centers on humanity's origin. Because what we think about our origins really matters.

As a case in point, let's consider the implications of human evolution, the prevailing scientific view of human origins. Scientific consensus claims that human beings emerged as the result of an evolutionary process that began 6 to 7 million years ago. Presumably, an apelike creature spawned an evolutionary lineage that culminated with the emergence of modern humans. Many scientists interpret hominids found in the fossil record—such as Lucy, *Homo habilis*, *Homo erectus*, and Neanderthals—as transitional forms documenting the evolutionary ascent of humankind.

If this origin story is correct, then human beings have no special status among all life-forms. We are merely one of a countless number of species that have existed throughout Earth's history. This point is powerfully illustrated in diagrams depicting the evolutionary tree of life for every major group of organisms thought to have existed throughout the last 3.8 billion years. In these diagrams, human beings are represented as just one small twig on one small branch of a sprawling evolutionary tree. We are an irrelevant part of life's vast evolutionary web.

The implications become even more troubling when we consider the nature of the evolutionary process. Biological evolution is unguided and historically contingent, without any direction or end goal. If human evolution is truly a fact, then there can be no ultimate meaning or purpose to human existence. This is the way evolutionary biologist Stephen Jay Gould described evolution's philosophical repercussions in his book *Wonderful Life:*

> This means—and we must face the implication squarely—
> that the origin of *Homo sapiens*, as a tiny twig on an improb-
> able branch of a contingent limb on a fortunate tree, lies well
> below the boundary. In Darwin's scheme, we are a detail, not
> a purpose or embodiment of the whole—"with the details,
> whether good or bad, left to the working out of what we may
> call chance." . . . *Homo sapiens*, I fear, is a "thing so small" in
> a vast universe, a wildly improbable evolutionary event well
> within the realm of contingency.[1]

This view of humanity is devastating, in my opinion. Because of science's influence and significance, the evolutionary account of human origins pervades cultures around the world. I contend that this view of humanity is responsible, at least in part, for many of the social ills that we see in our world today, including the rampant immorality present in every society. If human beings are merely animals produced by unguided, historically contingent evolution, then human life has no inherent value and people lack any dignity. If human evolution is true, then we are not accountable to a creator. We can do whatever we please.

In this chapter, I would like to provide a scientific response to the challenge represented by human evolution. I hope to show that the scientific case for human evolution is not open and shut. And, that there is scientific merit to a view that regards human beings as the product of a creator's handiwork, specially endowed with intelligence and the capacity for speech—qualities necessary for beings assigned as God's vice regents on Earth and that align with the image of God. A significant part of my response will focus on the role that philosophy plays in the operation of contemporary science.

Philosophy's Role in Science
Methodological naturalism provides the philosophical framework for science. This concept is distinct from philosophical naturalism, yet is related to it. According to philosophical naturalism, the material, physical universe is all that exists. There is no supernatural realm, no reality outside of the universe itself, and no God. As late astronomer Carl Sagan once quipped, "The cosmos is all that is or ever was or ever will be."

In contradistinction to philosophical naturalism, *methodological* naturalism claims to be metaphysically neutral on the question of God's existence. According to the tenets of methodological naturalism, when one engages in the scientific enterprise, it is necessary to suspend belief in God, regardless of one's personal convictions. Only natural, mechanistic explanations are allowed to account for the universe and its phenomena. One cannot appeal to the supernatural, but that doesn't mean the supernatural doesn't exist. Simply put, the supernatural is not given a place in the scientific endeavor.

In other words, even if you believe that God exists, your views cannot influence the way you do science. Methodologically speaking, you must function as if God does not exist. Sometimes methodological naturalism is called provisional atheism or benchtop atheism. This restriction makes methodological naturalism functionally equivalent to philosophical naturalism—rendering science an inherently atheistic enterprise, though its practitioners may well believe God exists.

In effect, methodological naturalism restricts the allowable explanations for the universe and phenomena within it such as the origin of humanity. Certain explanations are off the table, a priori. Consequently, intelligent design and creationism cannot be part of the construct of science. Any explanation stating that an intelligent agent is responsible for, say, the origin of humanity, is prohibited. As a result, human evolution is the only available alternative for someone who's trying to account for the origin of humanity—scientifically.

The net effect is that human evolution is scientifically true by default. No matter how much evidence exists challenging the evolutionary paradigm it cannot be supplanted because no other alternative explanation is allowed.

A statement by Harvard biologist Richard Lewontin powerfully illustrates methodological naturalism's grip on the scientific enterprise:

> We take the side of science in spite of the patent absurdity of some of its constructs, in spite of its failure to fulfill many of its extravagant promises of health and life, in spite of the tolerance of the scientific community for unsubstantiated just-so stories, because we have a prior commitment, a commitment to materialism. It is not that the methods and institutions of science somehow compel us to accept a material explanation of the phenomenal world, but, on the contrary, that we are forced by our a priori adherence to material causes to create an apparatus of investigation and a set of concepts that produce material explanations, no matter how counter-intuitive,

no matter how mystifying to the uninitiated. Moreover, that
materialism is absolute, for we cannot allow a Divine Foot in
the door.[2] (emphasis in original)

Many people claim overwhelming evidence for human evolution exists,
but I argue otherwise. Rather than rock solid science, the case for human evolution is largely philosophical in its construction. Essentially, many in the scientific community simply choose to interpret the scientific data from within
the evolutionary framework. Biologists claim that two lines of evidence make
the case for human evolution: (1) the hominid fossil record and (2) the genetic
similarities between humans and the great apes.

However, if one relaxes the restrictions of methodological naturalism, it is
possible to view the same data and evidence as fully compatible with a creation
model or intelligent design perspective.

The Fossil Record

As I mentioned earlier, many scientists interpret hominids—such as Lucy, *H.
habilis*, *H. erectus*, and Neanderthals—as transitional forms documenting the
evolutionary ascent of humankind.

But if this interpretation of the hominid fossil record is valid, then scientists should be able to do two things. First, we should find clearly established
evolutionary relationships among the hominids in the fossil record and, second, we should identify a clear evolutionary pathway leading to modern humans. And yet, neither of these criteria has been met. Evolutionary biologists
have no idea how human evolution proceeded—assuming it did at all.

Hominid Evolutionary Relationships
Consider the typical diagrams that depict some of the hominids found in the
fossil record and that attempt to show the evolutionary connections between
these different creatures (see figure 6). Diagrams like this often appear in textbooks on human evolution and in journal articles published in the scientific
literature.

The bars show the time frame when specific hominid species existed on
Earth. They are based on fossils recovered from the geological records and
represent actual data. Note the lines connecting the bars. They represent an
attempt to show the relationship between the hominids in an evolutionary
framework. If you examine the diagram carefully, you will see question marks
on each line. These question marks indicate uncertainty on the part of the

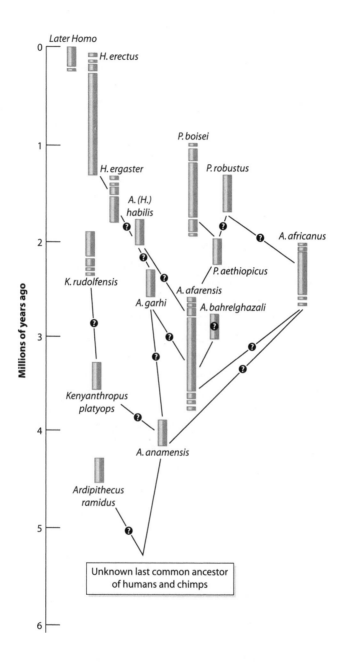

Figure 6: Presumed Evolutionary Relationships among the Australopithecines and Other Related Genera

scientific community about the precise evolutionary relationships of the different hominids. In fact, evolutionary diagrams produced by individual paleoanthropologists often differ significantly from one another, reflecting sharp disagreements over hominid evolution.

Chaos often ensues when researchers discover new fossil specimens or when an entirely new hominid species is identified. Instead of bringing resolution to the debates about hominid evolution, these new discoveries usually create greater dissension. It is not uncommon to read headlines that state: "New Hominid Find Rewrites Human Evolution" or "New Hominid Discovery Shakes Human Evolutionary Tree."

This chaos reveals how uncertain and speculative evolutionary interpretations of the hominid fossil record are. It raises questions about the evolutionary model's suitability as a framework for understanding the natural history of hominids. In science, new discoveries bring clarity and greater consensus to a valid theory, but they cause problems for an invalid theory, as is the case for human evolution.

The problems for human evolution are much more severe. Most of the available fossil data consists of craniodental remains. A few years ago two paleoanthropologists, Bernard Wood and Mark Collard, published a paper in which they showed that craniodental remains are inherently unreliable and of no use for building evolutionary trees:

> Little confidence can be placed in phylogenies generated solely
> from higher primate craniodental evidence. The corollary of
> this is that existing phylogenetic hypotheses about human
> evolution are unlikely to be reliable.[3]

In other words, the two researchers admit that it is impossible to know the evolutionary relationships that exist among the hominids, *even* if those relationships actually do exist. My question is, if we cannot know the evolutionary relationships that exist among the hominids, then how can we be confident that these hominids relate to each other through an evolutionary framework?

A Pathway to Modern Humans
Another serious problem arises when paleoanthropologists try to interpret the hominid fossil record from an evolutionary vantage point. They cannot identify a clear pathway through the fossil record that leads to the emergence of modern humans. In fact, paleontologists consider every hominid species

depicted as transitional forms in biology textbooks to be evolutionary side branches and dead ends, including:

- Neanderthals
- *Homo erectus*
  - Peking Man
  - Java Man
- *Homo antecessor*
- *Homo habilis*
- *Australopithecus afarensis*
  - Lucy
- *Australopithecus africanus*
  - Taung Child

The fact of the matter is that no paleoanthropologist knows how modern humans evolved. As a scientist, I question if we can confidently declare human evolution a fact if we cannot find the evolutionary path that led to human beings.

Another problem with interpreting the hominid fossil record from an evolutionary standpoint stems from the inability of paleoanthropologists to identify common ancestors. According to standard evolutionary models, *Homo heidelbergensis* is the last common ancestor for humans and Neanderthals, with Neanderthals and humans serving as representatives for two separate evolutionary branches.

Even though this is a prominent evolutionary model, it lacks supportive evidence. For example, based on some recent fossil finds, some paleoanthropologists now question the existence of *H. heidelbergensis*. If the species did not exist, then which hominid was the last common ancestor leading to humans and Neanderthals? This seems to be a serious problem.

Recently, a team of paleoanthropologists tried to reconstruct the last common ancestor by examining dental remains. They studied 1,200 fossil teeth and, from their analysis, constructed the tooth anatomy of the last common ancestor. To their disappointment, when they compared their reconstructions to dental remains recovered from the fossil record, no matches were found. In other words, they failed to identify the last common ancestor for humans and Neanderthals.

Paleoanthropologists have experienced similar failure for humans and chimpanzees. Many anthropologists think that the last common ancestor of humans and chimpanzees was a knuckle-walking apelike creature. According to this theory, the ability to walk upright (bipedalism) emerged when climate change transformed the woodlands of East Africa into an open savanna. Under these new conditions, bipedalism offered several advantages. Thus, a dramatic change in the environment served as the evolutionary driving force spurring on the emergence of bipedal capabilities among the hominids. Additionally, according to the standard model, the hand of the human-chimp ancestor underwent an evolutionary transformation from one that supported knuckle-walking to one that would eventually manipulate stone tools.

However, neither of these standard evolutionary stories matches the latest data. New discoveries indicate that bipedalism emerged in the woodland environment, *not* an open savanna. Also, the last common ancestor of humans and chimps possessed hands like those of modern humans, not knuckle-walking apes. In other words, the textbook descriptions associated with human evolution are incorrect.

Paleoanthropologists have no idea what the last common ancestor of humans and chimps looked like. In my view, if we cannot confidently identify common ancestors in human evolutionary scenarios, then skepticism about human evolution is justified.

And yet, despite these problems (and more) facing an evolutionary interpretation of human origins, paleoanthropologists will not entertain alternative models from a creation or intelligent design perspective because of the restrictions of methodological naturalism. Human evolution must be true—by default. Therefore, they interpret the hominid fossil record from within an evolutionary framework, regardless of the intractable problems associated with those interpretations.

So, how do we explain the hominids from a creation model or intelligent design standpoint? The RTB creation model regards hominids as creatures made by a creator for his purposes; these creatures existed for a period before going extinct. Hominids possessed some measure of intelligence and emotional capability—as do all animals—but they lacked advanced cognitive and spiritual capabilities.

Theists who are creationists can view these creatures as part of God's handiwork—a view that makes as much sense of the data as an evolutionary view. Later, I will argue that creationism makes even *better* sense of the data when defining features of humanity, such as language, are considered. But, at this juncture, I want to turn our attention to the shared genetics similarities between humans and the great apes.

Genetic Similarities between Humans and the Great Apes

Molecular biologists have sequenced the genomes of extant creatures including humans, chimpanzees, bonobos, gorillas, orangutans, and macaques. And using ancient-DNA technology, they have also sequenced the genomes of Neanderthals and the Denisovans. These data reveal a high degree of genetic similarities between humans, the great apes, and the hominids. In fact, evolutionary biologists can build evolutionary trees from the shared genetic features. To put it another way, biologists interpret the shared features as reflecting an evolutionary history and shared evolutionary ancestry.

When I interact with evolutionary biologists, I hear them say—time and time, again—that the only way to make sense of the shared genetic features is within an evolutionary framework. And I agree with them. If you embrace methodological naturalism as the framework for science, then the shared genetics provide compelling evidence for common descent. *However*, if you are willing to relax the restrictions of methodological naturalism, then there are other ways to interpret shared genetic features. For example, the shared biological features could be viewed as features designed using the same design templates.

In fact, there is a historical precedent for interpreting shared biological features as evidence for common *design*, not common *descent*.

Archetypal Designs

Prior to the publication of Charles Darwin's *Origin of Species*, many biologists interpreted shared biological features in organisms that naturally grouped together as variants of archetypal designs that existed in the Mind of the First Cause. In fact, Sir Richard Owen—the most preeminent biologist of his time—developed an elaborate theoretical framework to explain shared biological features that centered on the archetype concept. Owen defined the archetype as "that ideal original or fundamental pattern on which a natural group of animals or system of organs has been constructed, and to modifications of which the various forms of such animals or organs may be referred."[4] Owen concluded that the archetype implied a "deep and pregnant principle . . . some archetypal exemplar on which it has pleased the Creator to frame certain of his living creatures."[5] In Owen's view, the archetype existed only in God's mind and was manifested in the created order in the form of shared biological features. These features often reflected variations of the archetype.

For Owen, the archetype represented teleology of a higher order. In his presentation to the Royal Institution of Great Britain, Owen stated:

The satisfaction felt by the rightly constituted mind must ever be great in recognising the fitness of parts for their appropriate functions; but when this fitness is gained, as in the great-toe of the foot of man and the ostrich, by a structure which at the same time betokens harmonious concord with a common type, the prescient operation of the One Cause of all organization becomes strikingly manifested to our limited intelligence.[6]

In other words, Owen marveled at the ability of the Creator to simultaneously satisfy the organism's functional needs within the constraints of the archetypal form. Darwin owed a significant debt to Owen's thinking. Yet instead of accepting Owen's archetype, he replaced it with a hypothetical common ancestor.

It is possible to apply the concept of an archetype to shared genetic features. In fact, this is a project that we are undertaking at RTB. We are in the process of developing a genomics model that can explain similarities and differences in the genomes of organisms from a creation and intelligent design perspective.

But, what about all the junk DNA found in the genomes of human beings and the great apes? How is it possible to interpret genomes as the work of a creator, when they are made up of so much nonfunctional DNA?

Addressing the Issue of "Junk DNA"

There is a common perception that a vast proportion of any genome consists of nonfunctional junk DNA that is the vestige, or leftovers, of an evolutionary history. In fact, there are shared junk DNA sequences in corresponding locations of the human genome and the great ape genomes. Many evolutionary biologists argue that shared junk DNA sequences make sense *only* if those junk DNA sequences arose in the last common ancestor and persisted in the different evolutionary advantages that arose from this hypothetical creature.

Unfortunately for evolutionists, discovery after discovery in the last decade indicates that the various classes of junk DNA do have function. This revolution in molecular biology came to a head in the fall of 2012, when the ENCODE Project published its phase 2 results. At minimum, it appears that 80 percent of the human genome consists of functional DNA. Researchers expect the percentage to rise to nearly 100 percent as ENCODE's phase 3 results become available.

This is what Eric Green, director of the National Human Genome

Research Institute, said when the phase 2 results were published:

> During the early debates about the Human Genome Project, researchers had predicted that only a few percent of the human genome sequence encoded proteins, the workhorses of the cell, and that the rest was junk. We now know that this conclusion was wrong. . . . ENCODE has revealed that most of the human genome is involved in the complex molecular choreography required for converting genetic information into living cells and organisms.[7]

The human genome appears to be far more elegant and sophisticated than we could have ever imagined. It displays features that bespeak a creator's handiwork. With this new scientific insight in hand, we can now legitimately view even shared junk DNA sequences as reflecting common design, not common descent, because they serve the same purpose in the genomes of humans and the great apes.

The bottom line is that what naturalists tout as the most compelling evidence for human evolution can be readily accommodated within a creation model or intelligent design framework. It is due to fixed philosophical presuppositions that much of the scientific community refuses to allow for this interpretation of the fossil record and genetic similarities.

Additional Challenges to Human Evolution

It is interesting to me that many of human evolution's cornerstone ideas are falling by the wayside. For example, in his book *The Descent of Man* Darwin argued that the capabilities that we think make us unique as humans have antecedents in the great apes and that these features arose gradually through evolutionary processes. According to Darwin, "In a series of forms graduating insensibly from some ape-like creature to man as he now exists, it would be impossible to fix on any definite point when the term 'man' ought to be used."[8] To put it another way, we are different only in degree, not kind, from the great apes.

This view is changing. A growing minority of researchers now argues for human exceptionalism. They contend that human beings truly are different in kind, not just degree, from other creatures. One such researcher, Thomas Suddendorf, a psychologist who studies mental development in humans and animals to understand the evolution of the human mind, writes:

We reflect on and argue about our present situation, our history, and our destiny. We envision wonderful, harmonious worlds as easily as we do dreadful tyrannies. Our powers are used for good as they are for bad, and we incessantly debate which is which. Our minds have spawned civilizations and technologies that have changed the face of the Earth, while our closest living animal relatives sit unobtrusively in their remaining forests. There appears to be a tremendous gap between human and animal minds.[9]

Anthropologists think that our capacity for symbolism is what sets us apart from all other creatures. Only human beings can represent the world with discrete symbols. We combine and recombine those symbols in a near infinite number of ways to create alternate possibilities. The symbolism manifests in the form of language, art, music, and even body ornamentation. It is our capacity for symbolism that makes us exceptional as human beings. This insight undermines a central theme of the human evolutionary paradigm.

Evolutionary biologists contend that symbolism emerged through an evolutionary process. They argue that hominids such as Neanderthals or *H. erectus* possessed a proto-symbolism that gave rise to sophisticated symbolism found in human cultures. Yet, the archaeological record fails to support this claim. For example, anthropologists Ian Tattersall and Jeffrey Schwartz point out, "Among the Neanderthals, all claimed instances of early symbolism are strongly disputed, and for *Homo erectus*, there are no specific claims of this kind at all."[10]

Humans truly are unique and exceptional.

In my view, the one capability that exemplifies our exceptional nature as human beings is our capacity for language. The origin of language in human beings defies an evolutionary explanation. For example, researchers have come to the recognition that language appears suddenly with the first humans and coincides uniquely with modern humans. Also, the very first language employed by modern humans was as complex as contemporary languages. Two statements from recent scientific articles illustrate this insight. A researcher at MIT in the United States writes, "The hierarchical complexity found in present-day language is likely to have been present in human language since its emergence."[11] And elsewhere, another research team concedes:

> By this reckoning, the language faculty is an extremely recent acquisition in our lineage, and it was acquired not in the

context of slow gradual modification of preexisting systems under natural selection but in a *single, rapid,* emergent event that built upon those prior systems but was not predicted by them. . . . The relatively sudden origin of language poses difficulties that may be called "Darwin's problem."[12]

The origin of language defies an evolutionary explanation. Yet, the sudden appearance of complex language is exactly what I would expect if human beings are the product of the Creator's hand.

The Scientific Case for Adam and Eve

And finally, using the techniques of molecular anthropology, evolutionary biologists have stumbled upon an extremely provocative insight about humanity's origin. Molecular anthropology involves comparing similarities and differences in the structure of DNA molecules sampled from people around the world. Variations in the DNA structure reflect our genetic variability.

Employing numerous distinct genetic markers, molecular anthropologists have concluded that humanity originated recently (about 100,000 years ago) in a single location (East Africa) and from a very small population of individuals. This insight stands in sharp contrast to multi-regionalism, the prevailing view that has long been a mainstay of human evolutionary theory.

What are most provocative, however, are the results when mitochondrial DNA is used as a genetic marker. It turns out that every person on the planet can trace their origin back to a single ancestral sequence of mitochondrial DNA that many scientists think corresponds to a single female individual, dubbed "mitochondrial Eve" by the scientific community. And every man on the planet can trace his origin back to a single ancestral piece of Y chromosome that many today think corresponds to a single man, called "Y-chromosomal Adam." Could mitochondrial Eve and Y-chromosomal Adam be the Adam and Eve described in Genesis, the first book of the Torah?

So, must we accept human evolution as a fact? If we insist on methodological naturalism as the framework for science, then, yes, we can only deduce that human evolution holds true. But if we allow ourselves to relax the philosophical (nonscientific) restrictions on science, now we are free to admit that the data from anthropology supports the notion that human beings are God's exceptional creations.

Resources to Dig Deeper

Fazale Rana with Hugh Ross, *Who Was Adam? A Creation Model Approach to the Origin of Humanity*, 2nd expanded ed. (Covina, CA: RTB Press, 2015).

Kenneth Keathley, J. B. Stump, and Joe Aguirre, eds., *Old Earth or Evolutionary Creation? Discussing Origins with Reasons to Believe and BioLogos* (Downers Grove, IL: Intervarsity Press, 2017).

Fazale Rana and Hugh Ross, *What Darwin Didn't Know* (Covina, CA: Reasons to Believe, 2009).

Hugh Ross, *Navigating Genesis: A Scientist's Journey through Genesis 1–11* (Covina, CA: RTB Press, 2014).

Notes

Introduction – Establishing Common Ground with People of Different Faiths

1. It should be noted that the Technics and Science Research Foundation has published the full proceedings from the first conference. For more information on the first and second International Conference on the Origin of Life and the Universe go to: theoriginoflife.net.

Chapter 1 – The Origin and Design of the Universe

1. See "'A Universe from Nothing' by Lawrence Krauss, AAI 2009," YouTube video, 1:04:51, posted by Richard Dawkins Foundation for Reason and Science, October 21, 2009, youtube.com/watch?v=7ImvlS8PLIo#t=16m49s.
2. John D. Barrow and Frank J. Tipler, *The Anthropic Cosmological Principle* (Oxford: Oxford University Press, 1986), 253.
3. Francis Crick, *What Mad Pursuit: A Personal View of Scientific Discovery* (New York: Basic Books, 1988), 138.
4. C. S. Lewis, *God in the Dock* (Grand Rapids: Eerdmans, 1970), 53.

Chapter 2 – Why I Believe God Exists: A Biochemical Case for the Creator

1. Richard Dawkins, *The Blind Watchmaker: Why the Evidence of Evolution Reveals a Universe without Design* (New York: W. W. Norton, 1987), 10.
2. Cary Funk and Becka A. Alper, Religion and Science, Pew Research Center (October 22, 2015), pewinternet.org/2015/10/22/science-and-religion/.
3. Will Clifford, "DNA Computing: Meet Dr. Adleman," Youngzine (February 2, 2013), youngzine.org/news/technology/dna-computing-meet-dr-adleman.
4. Dawkins, *The Blind Watchmaker*, 7.
5. Dawkins, *The Blind Watchmaker*, 9.

6. Leslie Orgel, "The RNA World and the Origin of Life," in ISSOL '02 *Abstracts*, 39.
7. Leslie Orgel, "Self-Organizing Biochemical Cycles," *Proceedings of the National Academy of Sciences, USA* 97 (November 7, 2000): 12503–7, doi:10.1073/pnas.220406697.
8. Paul Davies, *The Fifth Miracle: The Search for the Origin and Meaning of Life* (New York: Touchstone, 1999), 131.
9. Simon Conway Morris, *Life's Solution: Inevitable Humans in a Lonely Universe* (New York: Cambridge University Press, 2003), 41.
10. Lin Jiang et al., "De Novo Computational Design of Retro-Aldol Enzymes," *Science* 319 (March 7, 2008): 1387–91, doi:10.1126/science.1152692.

Chapter 3 – The Inspirational Design of DNA

1. A Hamilton path is a trace through a graph in which the line passes through each vertex only once. The Knight's tour is a path through a chess board in which the knight visits each square only once.
2. William Paley, *Natural Theology or Evidence of the Existence and Attributes of the Deity, Collected from the Appearances of Nature*, Oxford World's Classics Edition, ed. Matthew D. Eddy and David Knight (New York: Oxford University Press, 2006), 7–8.
3. Kenneth R. Miller, "Life's Grand Design," *Technology Review* 97 (February/March 1994): 24–32.

Chapter 4 – Why Would a Good God Create Viruses?

1. This rate is for data from 2016, according to the World Health Organization (WHO), who.int/mediacentre/factsheets/fs286/en/.
2. Carl Zimmer, *A Planet of Viruses*, 2nd ed. (Chicago: University of Chicago Press, 2015), 48.
3. Zimmer, *A Planet of Viruses*, 105.
4. According to the WHO, fewer than 50 cases were reported in 2016: who.int/mediacentre/factsheets/fs114/en/.

Chapter 5 – Unequivocating Evolution

1. Relevant precursors of some L-amino acids and D-sugars, enriched with enantiomers, may be produced under simulated interstellar space conditions or under narrow and specific wavelengths of circular polarized light. Some enantiomerically enriched precursors and a few L-amino acids have also been detected on carbonaceous chondrites (meteorites) that have

fallen to Earth. Crystallization, through cycles of hydration and dehydration, suggests models where at least some biologically relevant amino acids and sugars may be amplified in relative levels of enantiomeric enrichment in the presence of other chiral compounds. (See Donna G. Blackmond, "The Origin of Biological Homochirality," *Cold Spring Harbor Perspectives in Biology 2* (May 2010): a002147, doi:10.1101/cshperspect.a002147; Donna G. Blackmond, "The Origin of Biological Homochirality," *Philosophical Transactions of the Royal Society B* 366 (October 27, 2011): 2878–84, doi:10.1098/rstb.2011.0130; Ronald Breslow and Zhan-Ling Cheng, "On the Origin of Terrestrial Homochirality for Nucleosides and Amino Acids," *Proceedings of the National Academy of Sciences, USA* 106 (June 9, 2009): 9144–46, doi:10.1073/pnas.0904350106; Ronald Breslow and Mindy S. Levine, "Amplification of Enantiomeric Concentrations under Credible Prebiotic Conditions," *Proceedings of the National Academy of Sciences, USA* 103 (August 29, 2006): 12979–80, doi:10.1073/pnas.0605863103; and Alexander J. Wagner et al., "Chiral Sugars Drive Enantioenrichment in Prebiotic Amino Acid Synthesis," *ACS Central Science 3* (March 21, 2017): 322–28, doi:10.1021/acscentsci.7b00085. However, the amount of starting material needed to produce such enantiomerically enriched products makes these models far less plausible.
2. B. Rosemary Grant and Peter R. Grant, "Evolution of Darwin's Finches," (Ernst Mayr Lecture am 4. November 2004), 424; edoc.bbaw.de/files/64/VII_03_Grant.pdf.
3. "An Interview with Michael J. Denton," produced by Access Research Network, Focus on Darwinism, published on December 5, 2014, video, 0:25, youtube.com/watch?v=B-Nh3RjZQil. An edited transcript of this interview is available at ukapologetics.net/aninterview.htm.
4. Romans 1:20 (NLT).
5. Antony Flew and Roy Abraham Varghese, *There Is a God: How the World's Most Notorious Atheist Changed His Mind* (San Francisco: HarperOne, 2007), 88.
6. Francis Crick, *What Mad Pursuit: A Personal View of Scientific Discovery* (New York: Basic Books, 1988), 13.

Chapter 6 – Human Origins: Common Design or Common Descent?
1. Stephen Jay Gould, *Wonderful Life: The Burgess Shale and the Nature of History* (New York: W. W. Norton, 1989), 291.
2. Richard C. Lewontin, "Billions and Billions of Demons," review of *The*

Demon-Haunted World: Science as a Candle in the Dark, by Carl Sagan, *New York Review of Books* (January 9, 1997), 31, nybooks.com/articles/1997/01/09/billions-and-billions-of-demons/.

3. Mark Collard and Bernard Wood, "How Reliable Are Human Phylogenetic Hypotheses?," *Proceedings of the National Academy of Sciences, USA* 97, no. 9 (April 25, 2000): 5003–6, doi:10.1073/pnas.97.9.5003.

4. Nicolaas A. Rupke, *Richard Owen: Biology without Darwin*, rev. ed. (Chicago: University of Chicago Press, 2009), 120.

5. Rupke, *Richard Owen*, 112.

6. Richard Owen, *On the Nature of Limbs: A Discourse*, ed. Ron Amundson (Chicago: University of Chicago Press, 2007), 38.

7. "First Holistic View of How the Human Genome Actually Works: ENCODE Study Produces Massive Data Set," NIH/National Human Genome Research Institute, *ScienceDaily*, posted September 5, 2012, sciencedaily.com/releases/2012/09/120905140913.htm.

8. Charles Darwin, *The Descent of Man, and Selection in Relation to Sex*, 2nd ed., Great Minds Series (1874; repr. Amherst, New York; Prometheus Books, 1998), 188.

9. Thomas Suddendorf, *The Gap: The Science of What Separates Us from Other Animals* (New York: Basic Books, 2013), 2–3.

10. Ian Tattersall and Jeffrey H. Schwartz, "The Evolution of the Genus *Homo*," *Annual Review of Earth and Planetary Sciences* 37 (May 30, 2009): 67–92, doi:10.1146/annurev.earth.031208.100202.

11. "The Rapid Rise of Human Language," Massachusetts Institute of Technology, *ScienceDaily*, posted March 31, 2015, sciencedaily.com/releases/2015/03/150331131324.htm.

12. Johan J. Bolhuis et al., "How Could Language Have Evolved?," *PLoS Biology* 12 (August 26, 2014): e1001934, doi:10.1371/journal.pbio.1001934.

Index

About the Author

Fazale "Fuz" Rana attended West Virginia State College and then Ohio University, where he earned a PhD in chemistry. His postdoctoral work was conducted at the Universities of Virginia and Georgia. He was a presidential scholar, elected into two honor societies, and won the Donald Clippinger Research Award twice at Ohio University. Fuz worked for seven years as a senior scientist in product development for Procter & Gamble before joining Reasons to Believe (RTB), where he now serves as vice president of research and apologetics.

He has published articles in peer-reviewed scientific journals, delivered presentations at international scientific meetings, and addressed church and university audiences in the United States and abroad. Fuz also coauthored a chapter on antimicrobial peptides for *Biological and Synthetic Membranes* in addition to contributing numerous feature articles to Christian magazines. He appears frequently on podcasts, vodcasts, and on television and radio interviews. Some of his books include *Origins of Life, The Cell's Design, Who Was Adam?, Creating Life in the Lab,* and *Dinosaur Blood and the Age of the Earth.* Fuz and his wife, Amy, live in Southern California.

About the Author

Anjeanette "AJ" Roberts is a research scholar at Reasons to Believe. She became a Christian at age twelve when she attended a concert at a local church where she became convinced of the gospel message of Jesus' atoning death and resurrection. Since then, AJ has been committed to seeking truth in science and Scripture and to sharing the great news of grace and hope found in Jesus Christ. AJ completed her BS in chemistry at the University of Tulsa in 1988 and her PhD in molecular and cell biology at the University of Pennsylvania in 1996. She conducted postdoctoral research at Yale University and served as a staff scientist at the National Institutes of Health, where she earned a Merit Award in 2005 for her contribution to research in infectious diseases. She joined the University of Virginia's microbiology faculty and directed graduate studies in microbiology, immunology, and infectious diseases from 2006 to 2013. She has coauthored over 40 articles published in peer-reviewed scientific journals and presented and lectured at institutions around the world.

In 2015, AJ joined RTB as a visiting scholar and, in 2016, became a permanent member of the RTB scholar team. Today, AJ puts her passion for truth to work engaging in science-faith topics such as evolution and design, integrating science and Christianity, and a theological perspective on viruses. AJ lives in Southern California with her faithful beagle, Chaim.

About the Author

Astrophysicist **Jeff Zweerink** writes and speaks on the compatibility of faith and science and on evidence for intentional design from multiverse theory, dark energy and dark matter, and exoplanets. His speaking engagements take him to universities, churches, and other venues around the country, including high school classrooms and church youth groups. Jeff also serves as executive director of Reasons Institute and Reasons Academy (RTB's accredited online learning programs), contributes to the ministry's vodcasts, podcasts, and blog, and hosts the RTB website's video interviews. He is the author of *Is There Life Out There?*, *Who's Afraid of the Multiverse?*, and coauthor of RTB's *Impact Events* student devotional series.

Jeff earned a BS in physics and a PhD in astrophysics with a focus on gamma rays from Iowa State University. Prior to joining RTB, Jeff spent much time working on the STACEE and VERITAS gamma-ray telescopes and was involved in research projects such as the Solar Two Project and the Whipple Collaboration. He still holds a part-time project scientist position at UCLA and is working on GAPS, a balloon experiment seeking to detect dark matter. Jeff is also a coauthor on more than 30 academic papers published in peer-reviewed journals, such as *Astrophysical Journal*, *Astroparticle Physics*, and *Astrobiology*, as well as numerous conference proceedings.

Jeff and his wife, Lisa, live in Southern California with their five children.

About Reasons to Believe

Uniquely positioned within the science-faith discussion since 1986, Reasons to Believe (RTB) communicates that science and faith are, and always will be, allies, not enemies. Distinguished for integrating science and faith respectfully and with integrity, RTB welcomes dialogue with both skeptics and believers. Addressing topics such as the origin of the universe, the origin of life, and the history and destiny of humanity, RTB's website offers a vast array of helpful resources. Through their books, blogs, podcasts, vodcasts, and speaking events, RTB scholars present powerful reasons from science to trust in the reliability of the Bible and the message it conveys about creation and redemption.

For more information, contact us via:
reasons.org
818 S. Oak Park Rd.
Covina, CA 91724
(855) REASONS | (855) 732-7667
ministrycare@reasons.org

WHAT YOU THOUGHT WAS SETTLED MIGHT NOT BE

"*Who Was Adam?* takes the creationist/evolutionist debate to a whole new level but insists on grounding the debate in the new evidences from genetics, biochemistry, archaeology, geology, and even astrophysics and the biblical narrative of creation."

– Walter C. Kaiser Jr.
President, Gordon-Conwell Theological Seminary

Visit reasons.org | RTB_OFFICAL 🅕🅨🅞🅓

Does believing in billions of years require a belief in evolution?

The entire Reasons to Believe scholar team gathers to discuss common questions about the integration of science and faith and whether God used evolution as a mechanism to create humans.

Visit reasons.org | RTB_OFFICAL

WHAT'S NEXT

We are here to empower you—so *you* can go out and empower others.

Reasons to Believe is here to help you sort through the evidence so that you can be confident in what you believe.

Visit **reasons.org/whatsnextbb** to access free faith-affirming resources.